15 PRACTICAL WOODWORKING PROJECTS

PERCY W. BLANDFORD

TAB BOOKS Inc.
Blue Ridge Summit, PA

TAB BOOKS Inc. offers software for sale. For information and a catalog, please contact TAB Software Department, Blue Ridge Summit, PA 17294-0850.

FIRST EDITION

FIRST PRINTING

Printed in the United States of America

Reproduction or publication of the content in any manner, without express permission of the publisher, is prohibited. No liability is assumed with respect to the use of the information herein.

Copyright © 1988 by TAB BOOKS Inc.

Library of Congress Cataloging in Publication Data

Questions regarding the content of this book
should be addressed to:

> Reader Inquiry Branch
> TAB BOOKS Inc.
> Blue Ridge Summit, PA 17294-0214

Contents

	Editor's Preface	v
1	Twisting Acrobat	1
2	Parson's Bench	4
3	Doll Carriage	8
4	Bookcase	14
5	Scooter	18
6	Riding Crane	21
7	Go-Kart	27
8	Swing Set	34
9	Rocking Chair	43
10	Dovetail Joints	48
11	Dovetailed Chest	58

12	Lathe Turning	62
13	Firehouse Armchair	70
14	Cheval Mirror	76
15	Tallboy	81
	Index	90

Editor's Preface

Despite the innovations of the past few years—electronic wonder toys and the advent of indestructible polystyrene furniture—wood remains the hallmark of quality, lasting beauty, and ruggedness, whether in a child's swing set or in the gracious lines of an early American tallboy. And no one translates wood's enduring strength and beauty into fun and functional items better than author and expert woodworker Percy W. Blandford.

Fifteen of Mr. Blandford's many projects are presented here for the weekend woodcrafter. From a simple acrobatic toy to a lathe-turned chair, we are confident that each project will present its own challenges and rewards, whether you are a beginner at the craft or already an expert woodworker.

The projects are taken from three of Mr. Blandford's numerous books on working with wood: *The Giant Book of Toys* (TAB book #1312); *The Master Handbook of Fine Woodworking* (TAB book #1247); and *How to Make Early American and Colonial Furniture* (TAB book #1114). Numerous other titles covering all aspects of the art of woodworking are available from TAB, both by Mr. Blandford and by many other fine authors.

So sharpen up the saw blades, get out the sandpaper, and set to work creating those heirloom-quality toys and furnishings that will be sure to be used, loved, and treasured now and for many years to come.

Project 1

Twisting Acrobat

This first project is a traditional toy with a long history, but it is still made and sold by European craftsmen (Fig. 1-1). The loosely jointed man hangs from a twisted string. By squeezing and loosening the two projecting ends at the bottom, he can be made to perform various tricks as the string twists or untwists. A problem with early examples was rapid wear on the string. Synthetic fishing line is now used, and it has a very long life.

Use a hardwood that is not brittle for the sides. The other parts can be of the same wood, or the body and limbs may be plywood. Make the two sides (Fig. 1-1A). Round their ends and mark the position of the bar, which will have to be held by two thin screws at each end. Cut the bar (Fig. 1-1B) with tapered and slightly rounded ends. There can be a very light cut across each side to provide a bed for the ends. Do not make this very deep, or it will weaken the side at the point where it gets most strain. Drill two holes ¼-inch apart near the tops of the sides for the fishing line; ¹⁄₁₆-inch diameter should do. Screw it into the bar; 2-gauge-by-¾-inch is a suitable size.

Draw the parts of the man—one body, two arms, and two legs—full-size from the drawing (Fig. 1-1C). Cut them out. If solid wood is used, place the grain lengthwise. Do some shaping by rounding edges if you wish, but the toy is quite effective with square edges. Drill the hands for the fishing line with the same size and spacing of holes as the frame sides. The other holes are for cotter pins, which

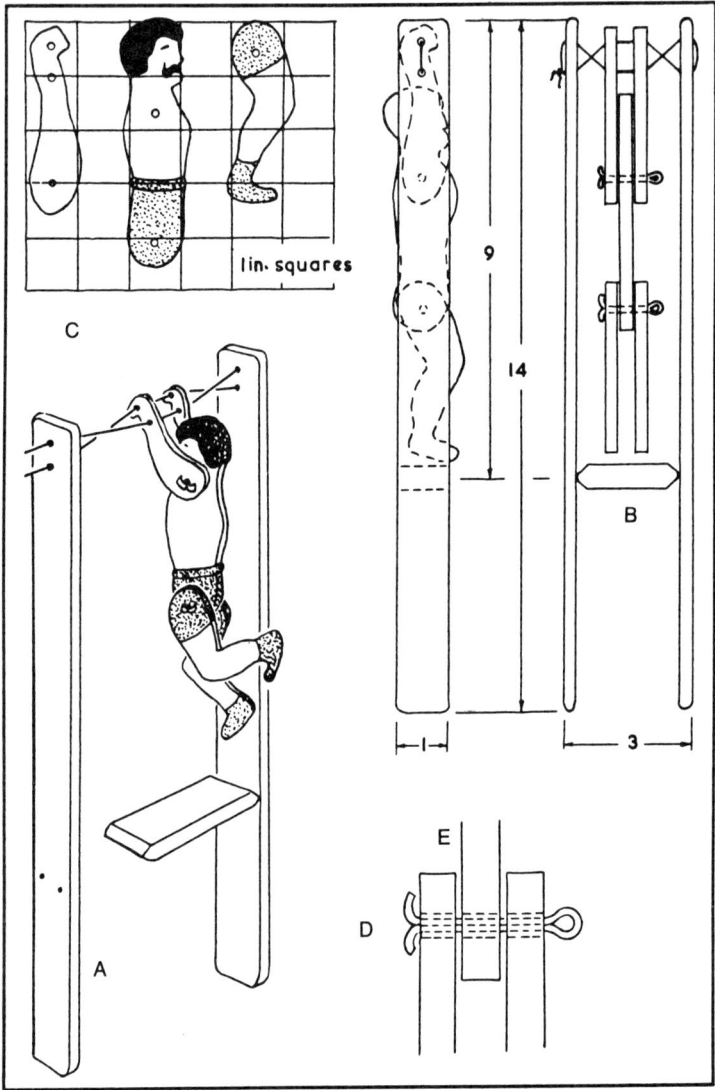

Fig. 1-1. This easy to make acrobat performs when the sides of his trapeze are squeezed.

may be ⅛-inch in diameter, but the holes should be oversize so the limbs can flop about (Fig. 1-1D).

Paint the parts of the man before assembly. You can give him facial details and indicate trunks and socks. Clear varnish all over will seal the colors, and it can also be used on the frame.

Assemble the man very loosely (Fig. 1-1E). Table knife blades held between the parts while you spread the ends of the cotter pins should give a satisfactory amount of play.

The fishing line you need is *monofilament.* It is a single piece and not several strands twisted together. The line is graded in pounds. The choice is not critical, but about 30-pound grade will do. Pass the line straight through without twists and temporarily tie the ends. Turn the acrobat over and over to twist the line. Squeeze the bottoms of the sides and see what happens. You may have to experiment with the amount and tension of the line to get the best results before finally knotting.

Materials List for Twisting Acrobat
2 sides	$1 \times 14 \times 3/8$
1 bar	$1 \times 3 \times 5/8$
a body from	$1 \times 12 \times 3/8$

Project 2

Parson's Bench

Our next project is a simple piece of furniture that serves multiple purposes. This handsome, functional bench will blend in nicely with any furniture style.

It can be made with one lifting top and the inside without a division, but dividing the inside and having two parts to the top allows one part to be opened without the other, and the support across the center prevents sag developing in the seat. Although the seat could be sat on directly, it would become more comfortable and more attractive if provided with fitted cushions for the top and back. With each made in two sections, one side could be opened without disturbing the other (Fig. 2-1A).

The front has its grain lengthwise, but the ends will be stronger if their grain is vertical. If there is much shaping to the arms, they will look better and be stronger if fairly thick—1 inch would be suitable—but if a simple rounding is all that is to be applied, they could be reduced to ¾ inch. Both back and front can be glued and nailed in place, or they could be extended enough to allow for dado joints (Fig. 2-1B). Dovetail joints are inappropriate since the vertical grain of the ends does not cut to make strong pins or dovetails. If dovetailed construction is preferred, the ends could be made cross grained and the arms made separately and doweled in place (Fig. 2-1C).

A central division can be fitted into dado slots. It is kept low enough to take a broader top to provide support under the meeting lids (Fig. 2-1D). In the original construction the division was probably nailed in directly without a dado.

The bottom shown is nailed underneath. Because this piece of furniture does not have to be carried about, maximum strength in the bottom is not so necessary. Bottoms were often made with the grain across the box and many boards used to make up the length (Fig. 2-1E). The projecting edges were rounded and blocks put under the corners to serve as feet. In a modern version, the main area of the bottom may be plywood, framed around with solid wood and the plywood rabbeted in, with the meeting edges covered by the box sides and ends.

The seat top is supported by battens across the ends at the same height as the center support. There is a rear strip full length at the back, nailed through the back and to the supports. The two seat parts that form lids rest on the supports and overhang the front slightly (Fig. 2-1F). It is advisable to put battens across to prevent warping, far enough in to clear the supports. The lids are hinged to the rear strip.

The upper extension of the back may be left straight or shaped. If it is to be hidden by cushions, it might as well remain straight. Too much shaping or carving should be avoided, in any case, as this could prove uncomfortable to lean against. A flowing curve to match the ends is suitable (Fig. 2-1G). Some of these seats had cut-out patterns in the back. Heart shapes were often used.

All exposed edges should be well rounded. The type of chest extended to a seat was common to many settlers, so the finish may be anything from a plain polish to painting with symbolic or pictorial decoration.

Materials List for Parson's Bench

1 Front	$15 \times 40 \times 1$	and 2 Arms	$17 \times 10 \times 1$
1 Back	$25 \times 40 \times 1$	2 Seats	$16 \times 19 \times 1$
1 Bottom	$18 \times 40 \times 1$	1 Seat rail	$3 \times 38 \times 1$
2 Ends	$17 \times 25 \times 1$	1 Division	$15 \times 17 \times 1$
or 2 Ends	$15 \times 17 \times 1$	3 Seat supports	$2 \times 17 \times 1$

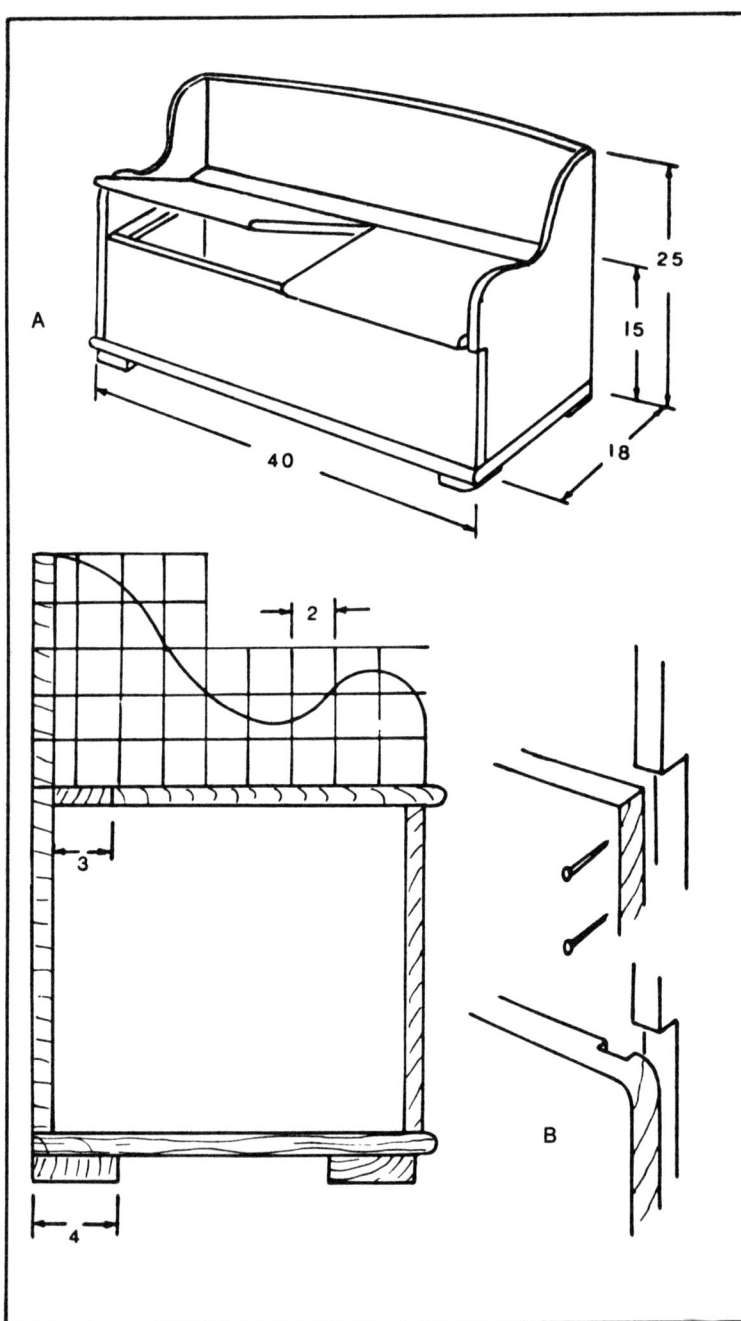

Fig. 2-1. A parson's bench can be used as storage as well as a seat.

Project 3

Doll Carriage

This is a strong carriage that is able to stand up to a youngster's rough treatment better than one modeled more closely on the usual full-size baby carriage (Fig. 3-1). The sizes shown (Fig. 3-2) should suit most girls, but it may be necessary to adapt them to fit a particular child, especially in the height and position of the handle.

Construction is shown with the main parts made of ⅜-inch plywood. The plywood has enough rigidity not to need stiffening along free edges. If thinner plywood or hardboard is used, strips of solid wood should be fitted along edges that are otherwise unsupported. The wheel frames might be ½-inch plywood, but it is unwise to use that thickness throughout. The result will be a heavy carriage.

The wheels shown are metal with rubber tires and diameters about 6 inches. They are mounted on axles ⅜ inch or ½ inch in diameter. Get the wheels and axles first, as wood sizes may have to be adapted if wheel sizes are very different.

Start by marking out the two sides (Fig. 3-3A). Fit ½-inch square strips at the ends above where the bottom will come (Fig. 3-4A). Allow for the wheel frames overlapping by 1 inch (Fig. 3-4B). Use glue and thin nails for assembly. Cut hollows in the top edges and round the corners (Fig. 3-4C). Make sure the opposite sides are properly paired and that their shapes match. Mark on the positions of the handles at 45 degrees to horizontal (Fig. 3-3B).

Mark out the wheel frames (Fig. 3-3C). See that their lengths match the carriage sides. It will help to get the shapes right if you

Fig. 3-1. A sturdy all-wood baby carriage will satisfy a young girl just as well as one made more like a full-size one.

make a template of half a frame, then use it to mark the parts each side of a centerline. Cut the outlines, clean off any raggedness, and round and sand the edges. Note that the hollow in the curve of the ends is needed to give clearance to the hood when it is lowered.

Cut the pieces for the ends and the bottom to the same width between the sides. The ends of the bottom and the top edges of the end pieces can be trimmed after assembly.

Glue and nail the ends between the sides. Put stiffening pieces across the bottom edges of the ends, planed to the angle of the bottom, and then put the bottom plywood in (Fig. 3-4D). Add the wheel frames inside the carriage sides close under the bottom (3-4E). Use glue in all meeting parts. Nail down through the bottom into the edges of the wheel frames before the glue hardens. Check that the whole assembly is square. Stand it level, under weights if necessary, until the glue has set.

The handle sides (Fig. 3-3D) are simple strips with rounded ends. Drill for the round rod deep enough for the joints to be glued and screwed from outside (Fig. 3-3E). Make sure that the distance between the sides match the overall width of the carriage. Fit the handles to the sides by screwing from inside or bolting through. These are joints that may be better without glue. If the handle height has to be altered as the child grows or another girl takes over, it can be done easily by redrilling.

Make a pair of hood sides (Fig. 3-3F). They will be better pivoting on bolts and nuts than on wood screws, so drill the hood sides and carriage sides for ¼-inch bolts. Mark on a side first where

9

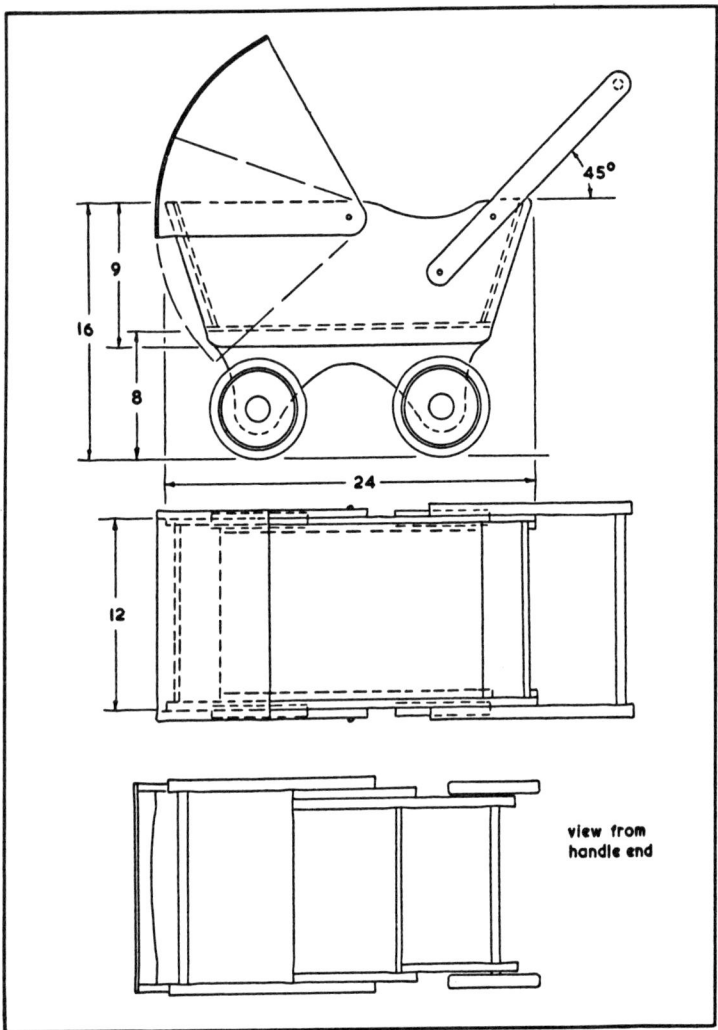

Fig. 3-2. Suggested sizes for doll's baby carriage.

the hood will come and mount it temporarily on the carriage side. Swing it to see that the finished hood will clear the corners and go low enough at the wheel frame.

The bottom hood frame piece is straight and nailed between the sides (Fig. 3-4F). The top piece can have its lower edge slightly hollowed and rounded in section (Fig. 3-4G). Make a temporary strut to go between the bolt holes while the hardboard is fitted. All of

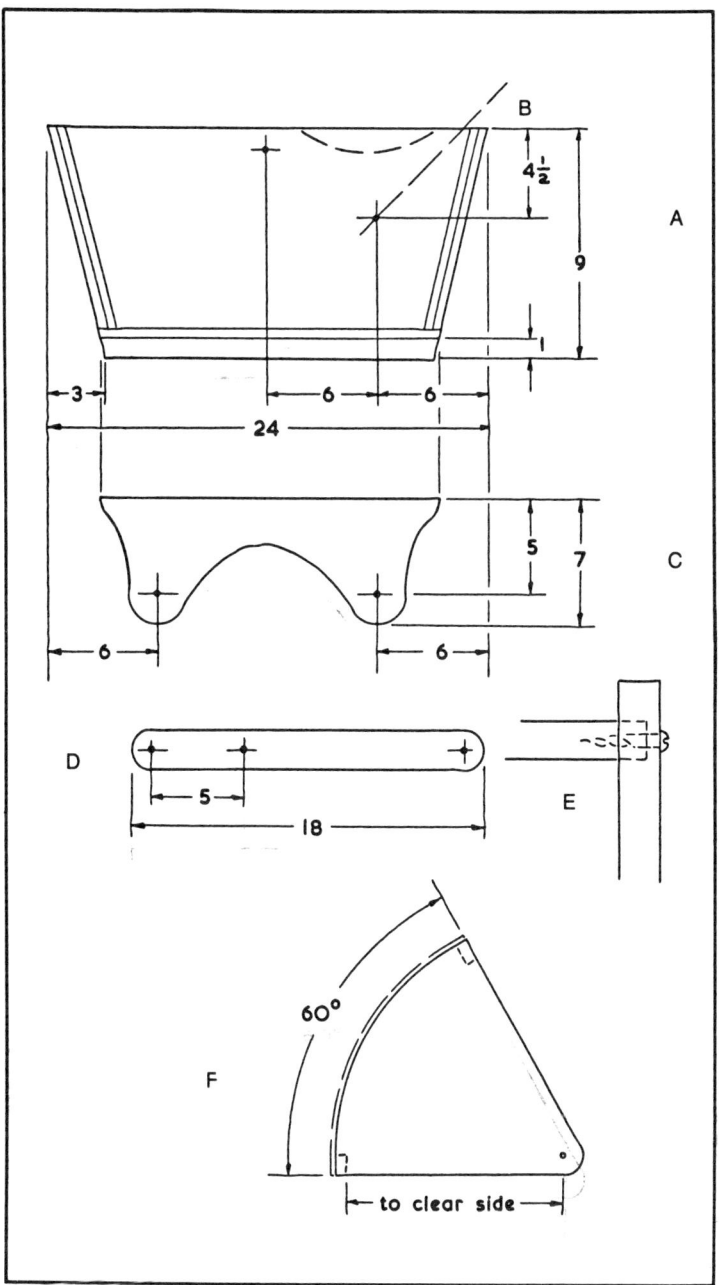

Fig. 3-3. Main parts of doll's baby carriage.

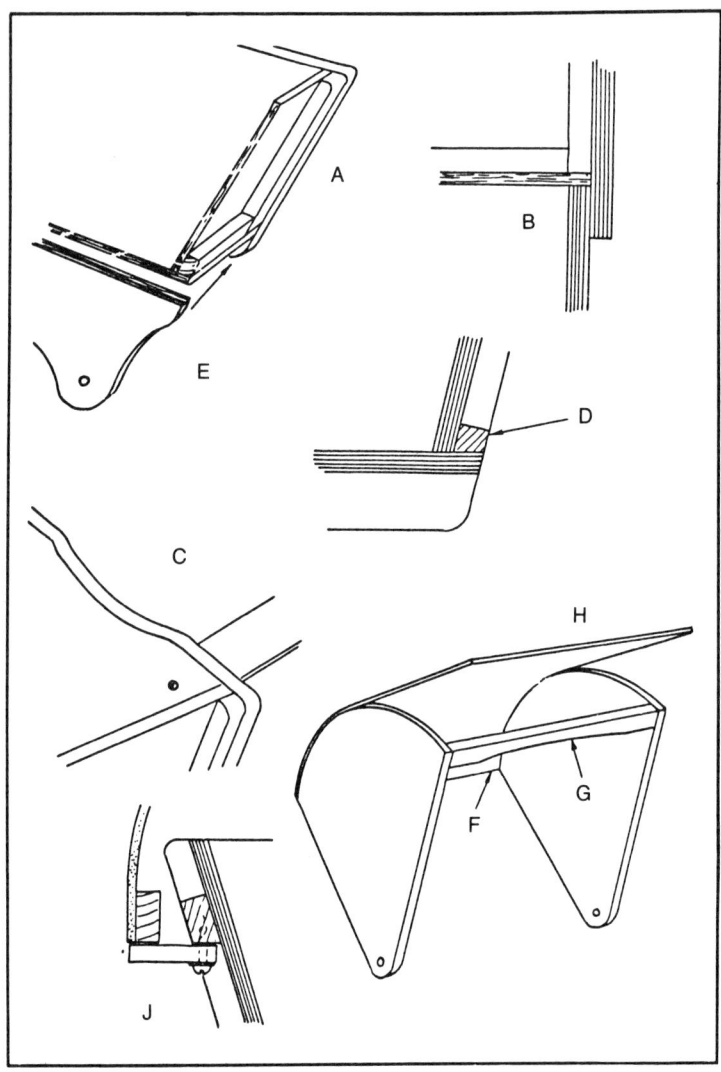

Fig. 3-4. Constructional details of doll's baby carriage.

the pieces across should be of a length that will allow the hood to swing with a little clearance over the carriage. Make up this assembly using screws through the bolt holes into the temporary strut.

Cut the hardboard piece slightly oversize. Spring it to shape. If this is difficult, moisten it. Have some clamps ready. Put glue on the meeting surfaces and start at the bottom edge with thin nails fairly closely spaced. Clamp to the bottom frame piece. Go around the curve with more nails (Fig. 3-4H) until you can nail to the top piece, where it is advisable to grip with more clamps until the glue has set. When this has happened, remove the clamps and trim the edges. Round all exposed parts, particularly corners. Try the hood in position after the temporary strut has been removed. See that its action is satisfactory.

The hood needs to be held up and be easy for a young girl to release and lower. Position a block of wood on the center of the end, with its lower edge level with where the hood should come when it is in the up position. Shape a short piece of wood as a turn button under it, pivoting on a screw with a washer under its head (Fig. 3-4J). Make it long enough to go under the end of the hood and around its end. It can be swung back when the hood is to be lowered.

Finish the hood and handles in bright colors different from those of the rest of the carriage.

Materials List for Doll Carriage

2 sides	$9 \times 24 \times 3/8$ plywood
2 ends	$9 \times 12 \times 3/8$ plywood
1 bottom	$12 \times 20 \times 3/8$ plywood
2 wheel frames	$7 \times 20 \times 3/8$ plywood
2 hood sides	$13 \times 15 \times 3/8$ plywood
2 handles	$1 1/2 \times 18 \times 3/4$
2 hood frames	$1 \times 13 \times 1/2$
framing from	$1/2 \times 60 \times 1/2$
1 handle	$5/8 \times 15$ round rod
1 hood	$14 \times 30 \times 1/8$ hardboard

Project 4

Bookcase

The same, simple woodworking techniques used in the previous project are here turned to the creation of an elegantly simple Early American bookcase. The design features a larger, deeper bottom shelf for big, heavy volumes (Fig. 4-1).

The bookcase can have plain outlines or the edges can be given rounded decoration. This is particularly suitable for the coarser-grained hardwoods such as oak, which gives an impression of solidity, and this is further emphasized by the projecting plinth (Fig. 4-2).

Mark out the 8-inch wide piece for the sides together with the positions of the shelves. Prepare the side extension pieces (Fig. 4-3A). Make sure all saw marks are removed from the tapered parts before gluing these pieces to the wide boards. Make sure the two sides match. It is advisable to leave some excess length at the bottom to trim level after gluing. It should be sufficient to glue and clamp the planed edges, but there can be dowels or secret screws to strengthen the joints. For the sake of a uniform appearance, the angle of the side extensions should be repeated at the top and on the back. Set an adjustable bevel to the angle and use this to mark the other bevels.

The shelves fit into stopped dadoes, with screws under the front edges. Although the bottom shelf must be the full width, the one above the wide compartment need not reach the front. It can be fitted without notching ½-inch back from the edge (Fig. 4-3B).

Fig. 4-1. Deeper, larger shelves are featured for big volumes.

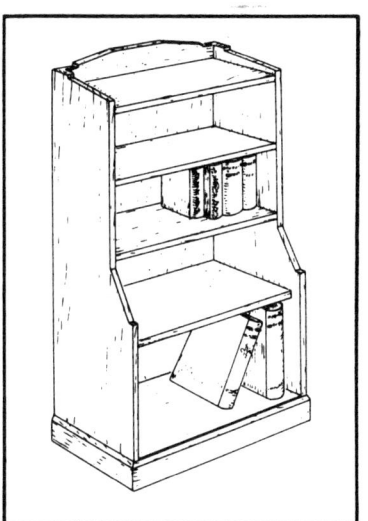

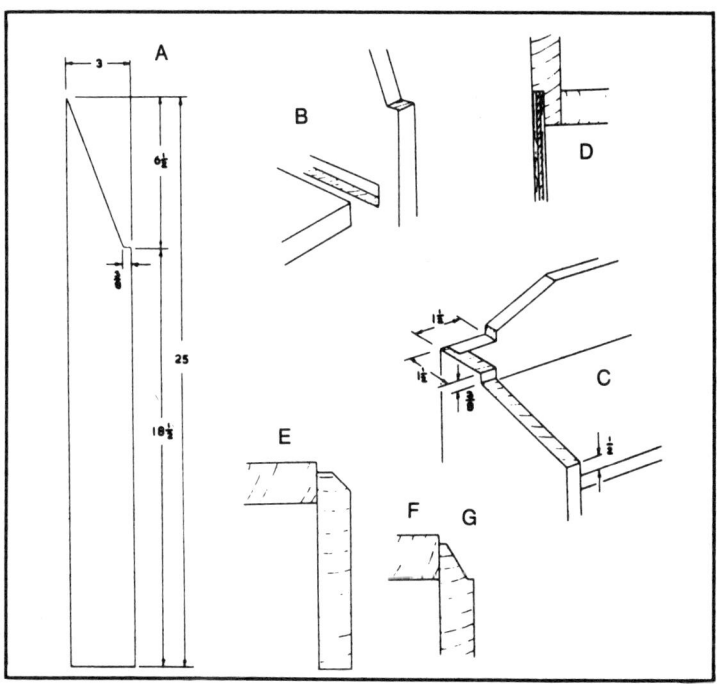

Fig. 4-2. Constructional details of bookcase: (A) side extension pieces; (B) fit the shelves; (C) prepare back; (D) rabbet back edges; (E) below shelf level; (F) plain bevel; (G) stepping down.

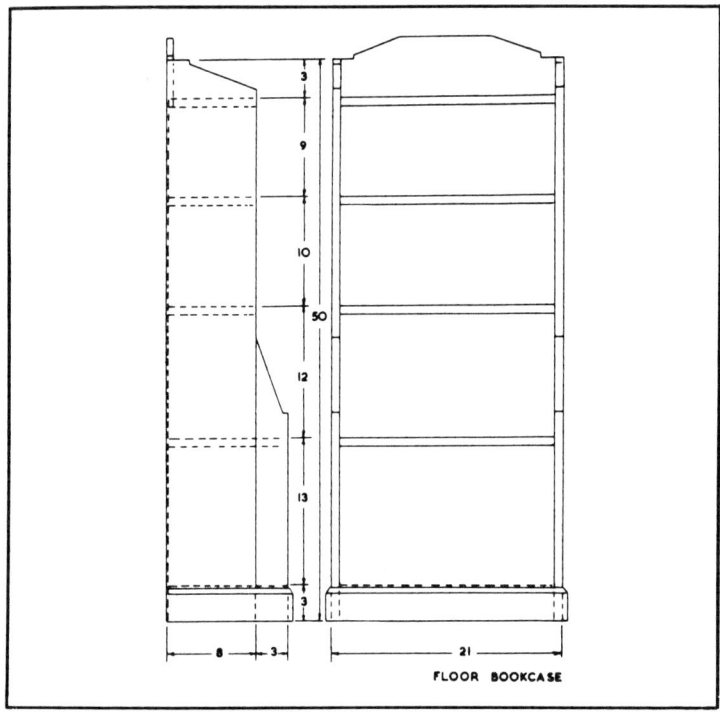

Fig. 4-3. Graduating shelf spacing gives a more pleasing appearance.

Shape the tops of the sides and prepare the back (Fig. 4-3C). Cut recesses for the back to come behind the top shelf. Rabbet the back edges (Fig. 4-3D).

Assemble the sides and shelves after sanding inner surfaces. Fit the top back. When the glue on these parts has set, cut the plywood to size and fit it into the rabbet with glue and fine nails. Do the same to the backs of the shelves and the rabbeted top piece.

Prepare the strips to make the plinth so that the width allows the top edge to come about ⅛ an inch below the shelf level (Fig. 4-3E). Give the top edge a plain bevel (Fig. 4-3F). Stepping it down (Fig. 4-3G) would give a section matching the other decoration, but being low and small it might not show. Miter where the plinth parts meet. If the bookcase is to go against a wall, cut the rear ends level with the back. If it is to stand away from a wall, make a rear piece of plinth and miter all corners. Attach the plinth with glue and a few screws from inside or with fine nails driven from outside and punched so that they can be covered with plastic wood filler.

Check the squareness of the bottom edges, otherwise the bookcase will not stand upright. It will help to plane each side of the bottom slightly hollow so that the weight is taken at the corners.

Materials List for Bookcase.

2 sides	$8 \times 51 \times 5/8$
2 side extensions	$3 \times 26 \times 5/8$
3 shelves	$7\tfrac{3}{4} \times 21 \times 5/8$
2 shelves	$10\tfrac{3}{4} \times 21 \times 5/8$
1 top back	$6 \times 21 \times 5$
1 plinth	$2\tfrac{7}{8} \times 23 \times 1/2$
2 plinths	$2\tfrac{7}{8} \times 12 \times 1/2$
1 back	$21 \times 48 \times 1/4$ ply

Project 5

Scooter

This scooter is almost entirely of wood and can be built in an afternoon. It can be fitted with a small sidecar, so a doll or other toy can be transported.

The design allows for wheels about 5 inches in diameter, mounted on suitable iron rods as axles. Get the wheels and make the axles before starting on the woodwork, so the sizes can be adjusted if necessary. Before cutting any of the wood, set out the front bottom corner full-size so as to get the sizes right. The handle should come at about 80 degrees to the platform.

Make the bracket that will carry the pivot with its grain following the longer direction (Fig. 5-1A). At the bottom, allow enough to project through the platform, so fillets can be glued in (Fig. 5-1B) to stiffen the joint. Make the platform (Fig. 5-1C) notched at the forward end to take the bracket, and cut away enough at the rear for the wheel. Glue and screw a thickening piece below the rear end (Fig. 5-1D). Drill through for the axle. Glue the bracket in place. Drive long screws or nails across it through the platform. Glue and nail fillets above the joint and add others below when you make the joint (Fig. 5-1E). See that the bracket is kept square to the surface of the platform when viewed from the front.

The upright handle is made in a very similar way to the platform, with the bottom cut away and thickened to take the wheel and axle (Fig. 5-1F). At the top, the best joint for adding the handlebar is a mortise and tenon (Fig. 5-1G). Keep the handlebar square where

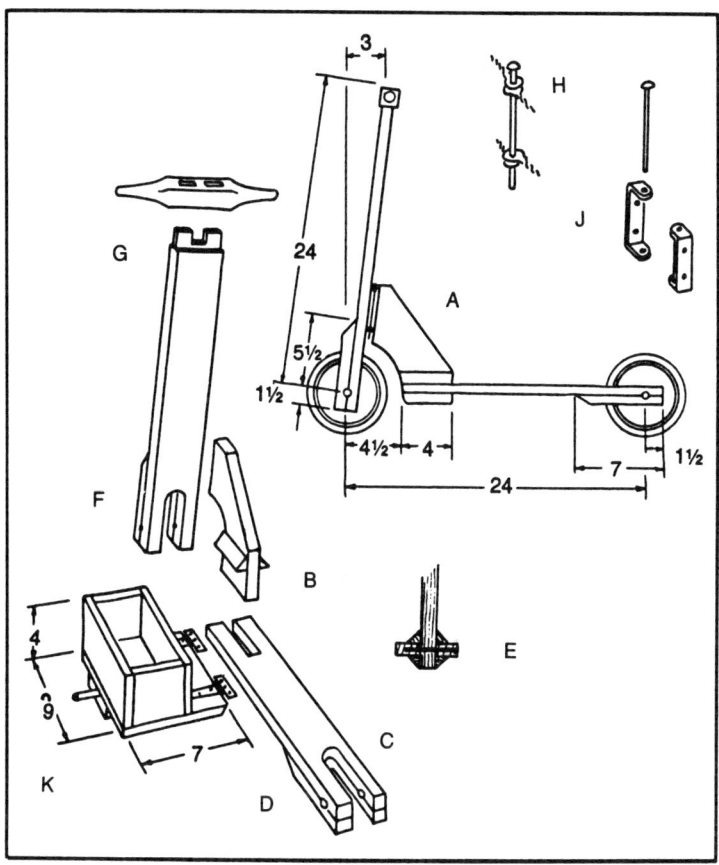

Fig. 5-1. This scooter can be fitted with a sidecar for toys.

it comes over the upright, but thoroughly round the projecting parts to form grips.

The simplest form of pivot is made with four large screw eyes and a rod or piece of a large nail through them (Fig. 5-1H). Another hinge can be made with two pieces of strip iron, about 1-inch-by-⅛-inch section, bent to interlock and drilled for screws or bolts into the woodwork (Fig. 5-1J).

A sidecar cannot be very large, or it may interfere with the foot that kicks against the ground. A simple box with its bottom extended is shown in Fig. 5-1K. Mount an axle with a block of wood underneath. At the edge next to the platform, bevel the underside to allow for tilting as the scooter is used. Attach the sidecar with two small T hinges.

Materials List for Scooter

1	platform	5 × 20 × ¾
1	bracket	6 × 14 × 1
1	handle	5 × 24 × ¾
1	handlebar	1¼ × 18 × 1¼
2	thickeners	5 × 7 × ¾
1	sidecar bottom	7 × 9 × ¾
2	sidecar sides	4 × 9 × ⅝
2	sidecar ends	4 × 5 × ⅝

Project 6

Riding Crane

This crane provides a riding toy suitable for a smaller child (Fig. 6-1). The more intricate design of the all-wood working parts should prove challenging to the craftsman.

The crane is mounted on furniture casters. The youngster can use his or her feet to propel it about the floor while lifting and moving loads. The child's weight on the rear platform provides stability, while he or she can alter the angle of the *jib* with one handle and lift loads with the other. *Pawls* on ratchet wheels give the young engineer more levers to move. The toy should be strong enough to stand up to normal use. With a child sitting astride it, there should be no fear of it toppling with any load he or she tries to lift.

Some of the parts are plywood, but the control tower is solid wood. Round parts can be made from dowel rods. The four casters are the type intended to be attached with screws. They should be obtained at the start, so any adjustment of size can be arranged to suit them. The type of caster with a stem to go into a leg cannot be used.

The general drawing (Fig. 6-2) shows overall sizes. If you decide on variations, they will affect some of the information in the detail drawings.

Start by making the base (Fig. 6-3A) from ½-inch plywood. Round the rear corners and edges. Mark on the position of the control tower. Put blocks underneath for the casters. The blocks

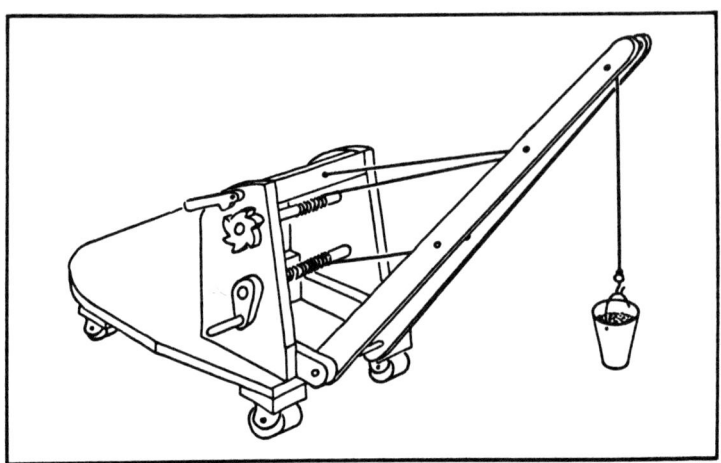

Fig. 6-1. Crane has a base on which children can sit while picking up a load.

must be large enough to take their mounting plates and spread widely for stability.

Mark out the control tower sides (Fig. 6-3B) and make them to match. Drill through for the ⅝-inch dowel rod winding drums. Make the jib supports (Fig. 6-3C) and the two crosswise pieces (Fig. 6-3D). Drill a small hole centrally in the top piece to take the end of a cord. Join these parts with glue and nails or screws. Mount the assembly on the base with the jib supports projecting forward over the edge.

The jib sides look best if they are given a curved taper towards the top (Fig. 6-4A). Mark them to take a spacing block at the bottom. A short length of dowel rod serves as a spacer where the tops are pulled in (Fig. 6-4B). Make the width of the spacing block to let the assembly be an easy fit between the jib supports.

The other three crosswise pieces shown serve as guides for cords. They can be pieces of ¼-inch dowel rod, but it might be better to make them of round iron rod about ³⁄₁₆-inch in diameter, which can be cut from large nails. The lifting cable goes under the lower one, then over the top one and down to the load. The jib-adjusting cable goes around the middle one and back to the hole in the top piece of the control tower. The jib can pivot on another similar iron rod, or there can be screws through the supports into the end of the jib.

Make the two winding drums overlong at first (Fig. 6-4C). Drill a hole in each to take the knotted end of the cord. If the ratchet

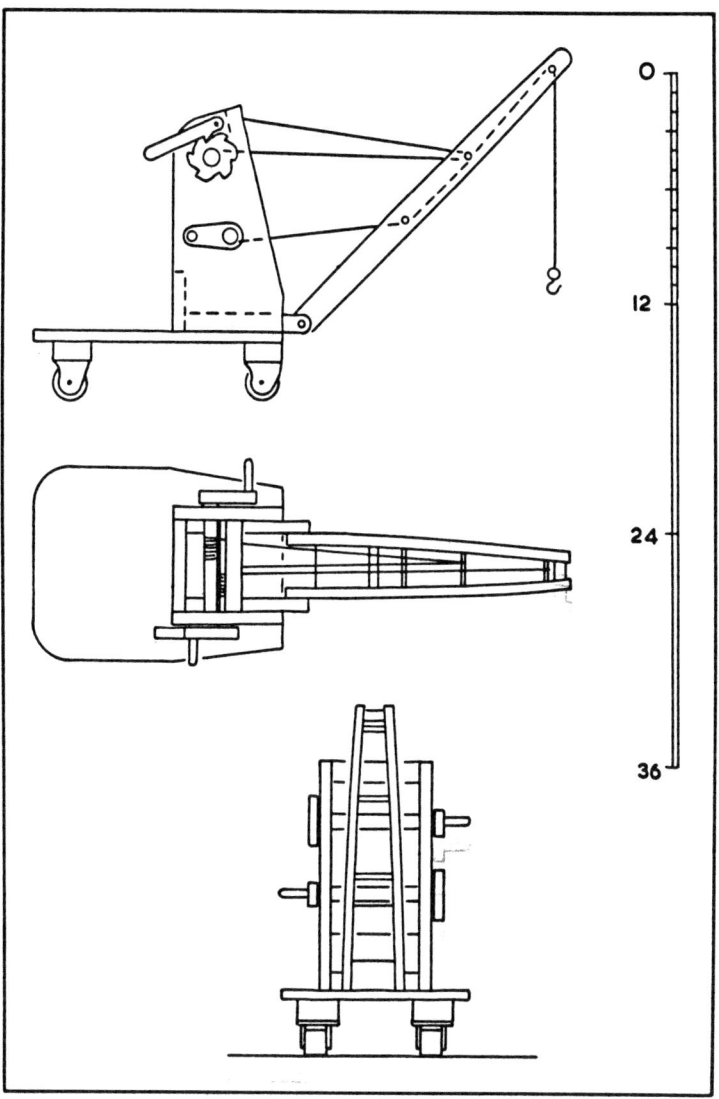

Fig. 6-2. Three views showing suitable sizes for crane.

wheels are glued on, the crank handles can be held with screws only, so it will be possible to withdraw the drums if necessary later. Make the crank handles (Fig. 6-4D) from plywood, unless you have some close-grained hardwood that will resist splitting. Glue in a piece of thinner dowel rod for the grip.

23

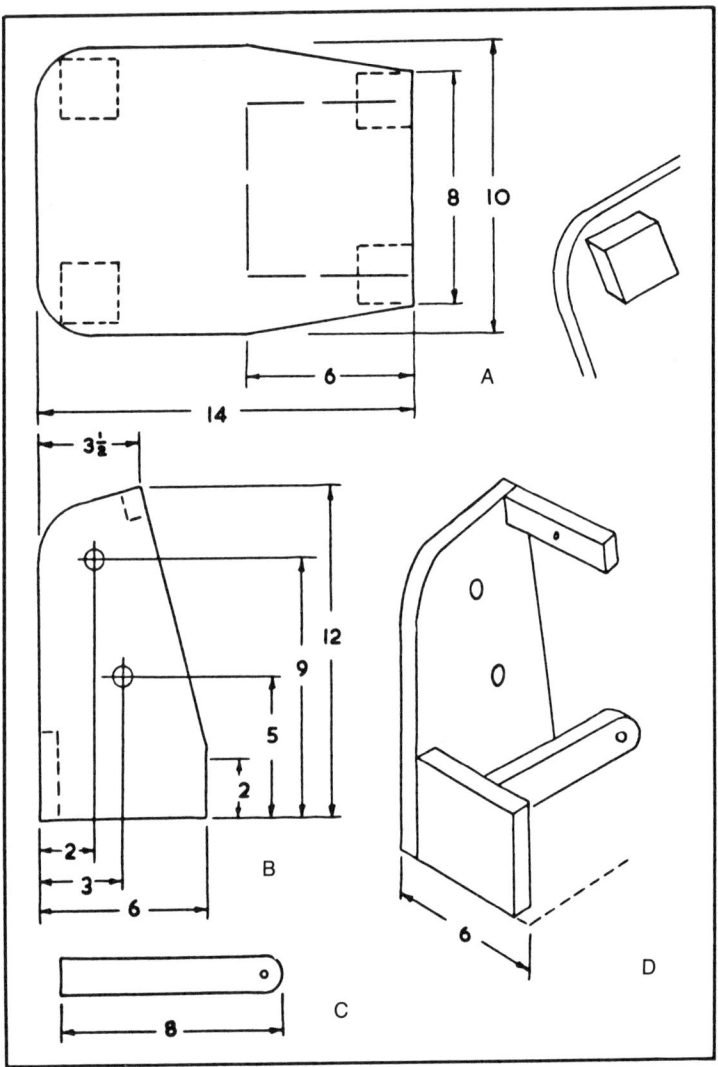

Fig. 6-3. Main parts of crane assembly.

The ratchets should also be of plywood. There can be any number of equally spaced teeth, but it is convenient to divide the circumference into six by stepping off the radius around it (Fig. 6-4E). Mark and cut the teeth evenly. The radial edges of the circle are most important. It may be sufficient to merely glue a ratchet wheel to the end of its dowel, but the joint can be tightened by putting

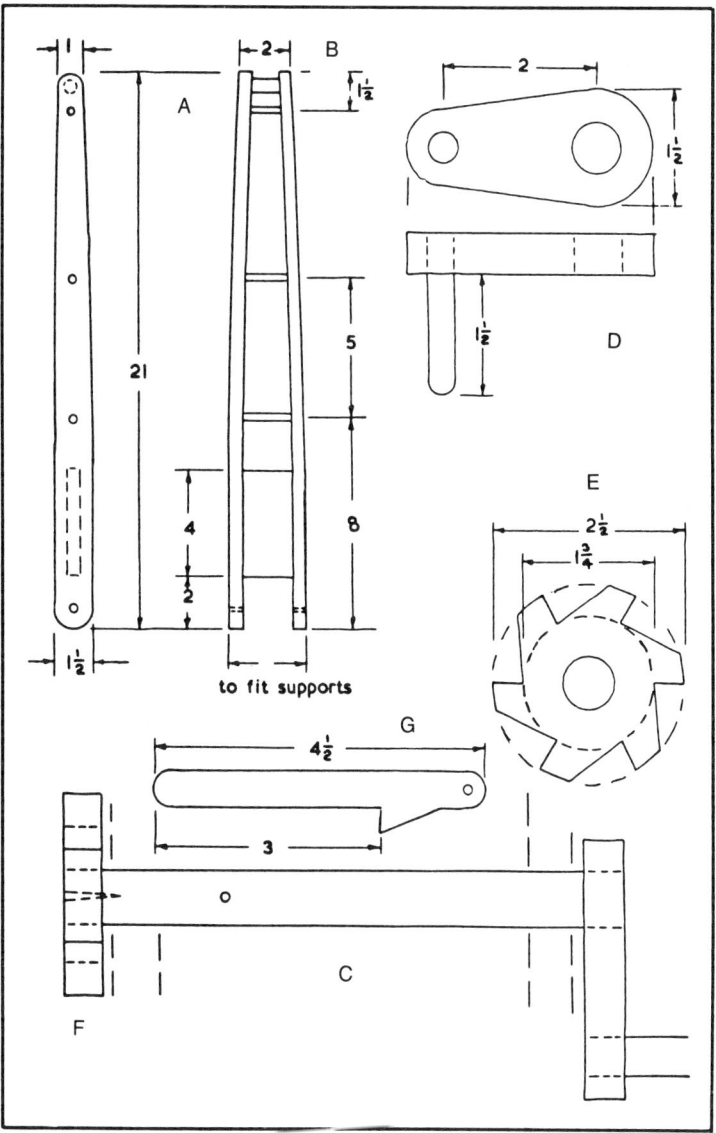

Fig. 6-4. Jib and parts of crane's mechanisms.

a saw cut across the dowel so a wedge can be tapped in as the joint is glued (Fig. 6-4F). Trim the end level when the glue has set.

The pawls (Fig. 6-4G) can be plywood or hardwood. The projecting pieces should fit against the radial teeth of the ratchet wheels and be given enough clearance to go easily into the spaces. Round the lever ends and drill the other ends for pivot screws. When the parts are assembled, locate each pawl where it can drop into the ratchet wheel and be lifted clear when the drum is to be reversed. Put washers between the handles and ratchet wheels and the sides of the control tower. Make a trial assembly, then dismantle the rotating parts for painting.

The cord that controls the jib angle should be only long enough to let the jib go out to about 30 degrees to the floor, so the user will not be troubled by the jib dropping out of control. He or she will then be able to wind it up to nearly vertical. Similarly, make the winding cable long enough to reach the floor when the jib is at its highest. It helps to have some weight at the hook, so it hangs down even when there is nothing on it. The hook can be bent from wire. A metal or plastic ball can be threaded on the cord above it as a weight.

Materials List for Riding Crane

1 base	$10 \times 14 \times \frac{1}{2}$ plywood
4 caster blocks	$2 \times 2 \times 1$
2 sides	$6 \times 12 \times \frac{5}{8}$
1 back	$3 \times 5 \times \frac{5}{8}$
1 top	$1 \times 5 \times \frac{5}{8}$
2 jib supports	$1\frac{1}{2} \times 8 \times \frac{5}{8}$
2 jib sides	$1\frac{1}{2} \times 21 \times \frac{1}{2}$
1 jib spacer	$2\frac{1}{2} \times 4 \times \frac{5}{8}$
Handle and ratchet	$\frac{1}{2}$ plywood
2 winding drums	$\frac{5}{8} \times 8$ round rod
2 pawls	$\frac{3}{4} \times 5 \times \frac{1}{2}$

Project 7

Go-Kart

Many children try to make themselves some sort of toy to ride on when they find discarded wheels and axles. The results are often crude and may be dangerous. This toy is intended to be a more craftsmanlike version of what they are trying to achieve. It has to be based on available wheels and axles, so sizes may have to be adjusted to suit. The go-kart shown (Fig. 7-1) is based on 6-inch diameter wheels and axles about 3/8 inch diameter. Rod may be cut for axles. The wheels can be secured by drilling the ends to take split pins. If there are existing axles with fitted ends, the width of the kart will have to be adjusted to suit. The seat should be wide enough to take the child, but not so wide that he can slide far sideways. Check his leg length. He steers with his feet while his legs are slightly bent. To give him control, his back should then be pressed against the seat back. If the go-kart is to be used for different children, or if it will have to accommodate the same child after he has grown, the chassis can be made longer than originally necessary. A hole for the pivot can be put nearer the seat to suit shorter legs. Then it can be moved to another position as the child's legs get longer.

The chassis has to take the main loads, so choose a strong board without flaws like cracks or knots. Taper to the front (Fig. 7-2A) to give foot clearance and round the edges. Notice that the front projects forward of the footrest. This is to give maximum bearing

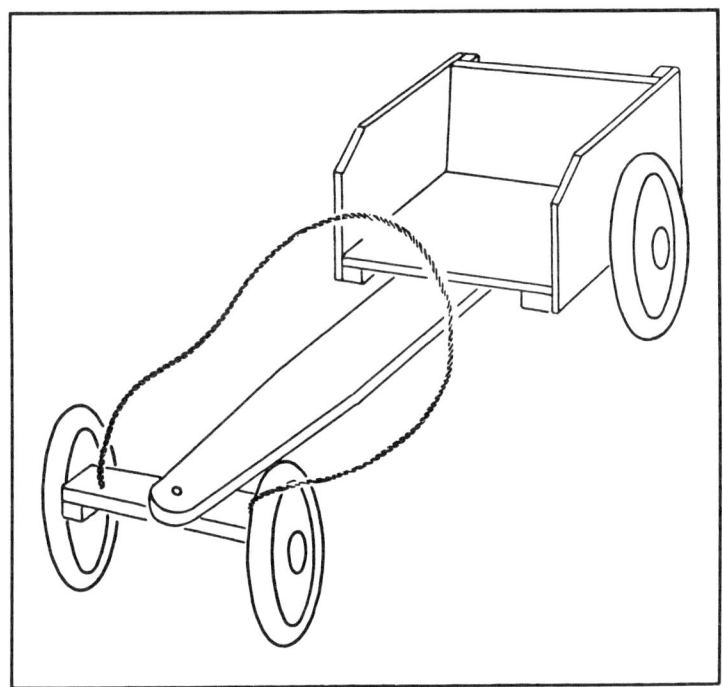

Fig. 7-1. Go kart has great appeal for children.

surfaces between the moving parts. On poorly made karts, slackness developing due to wearing surfaces is a common weakness.

The footrest also supports the front axle (Fig. 7-2B). Arrange blocks under its ends, so they can be drilled for the axle (Fig. 7-3A). Mark and drill the two blocks before attaching them, so the holes match and are drilled squarely. Put two pieces of ¾-inch square strip across the tops to act as outer foot stops and keep feet away from the wheels (Fig. 7-3B).

The pivot is a bolt, about ½-inch diameter, with its head underneath. It can be either a square neck coach bolt or a plain head bolt with a washer. Arrange a large washer above the chassis. Either use lock nuts or tighten two ordinary nuts against each other to lock them (Fig. 7-3C). If you do not, the assembly will soon develop a wobble. The alternative to direct rubbing is to make a sheet metal or thin plywood washer as large as the bearing surfaces.

The seat is boxlike and mounted on the top of the chassis. It can be made of solid wood, but it is shown as comprised of plywood stiffened at the joints (Fig. 7-2C). Cut the bottom and put the

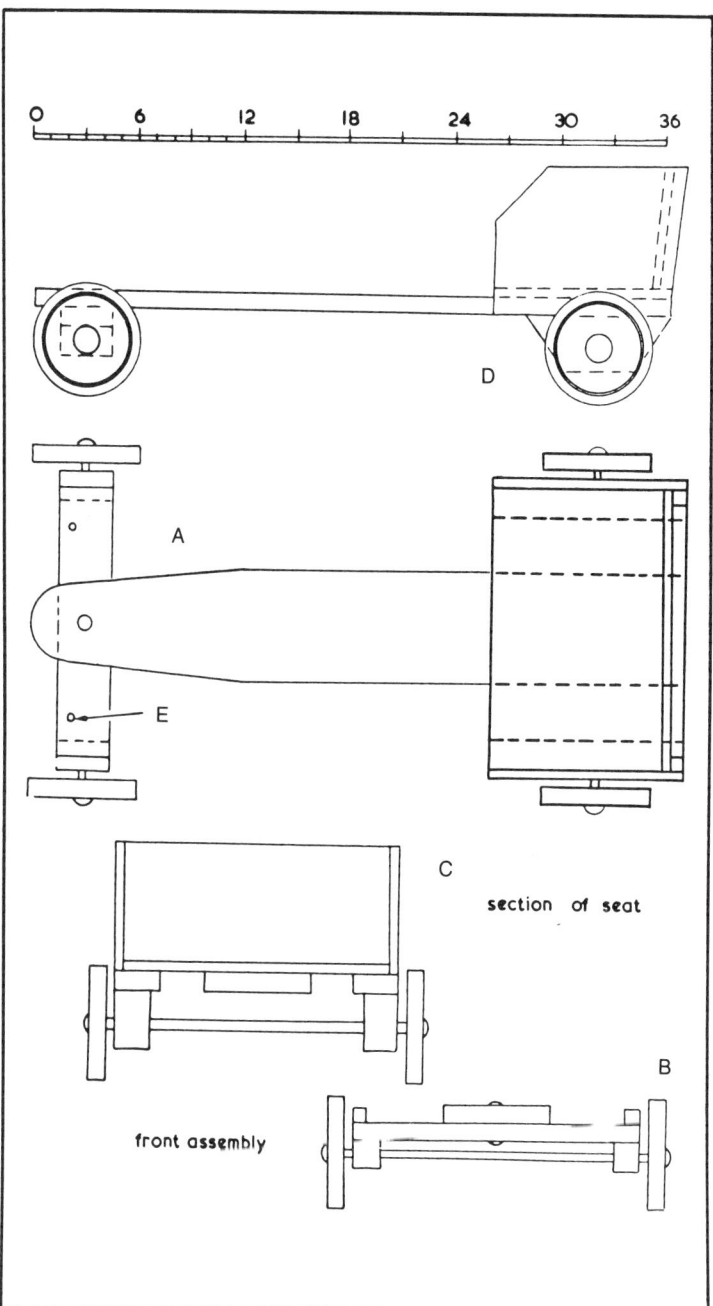

Fig. 7-2. Suitable sizes for go-kart.

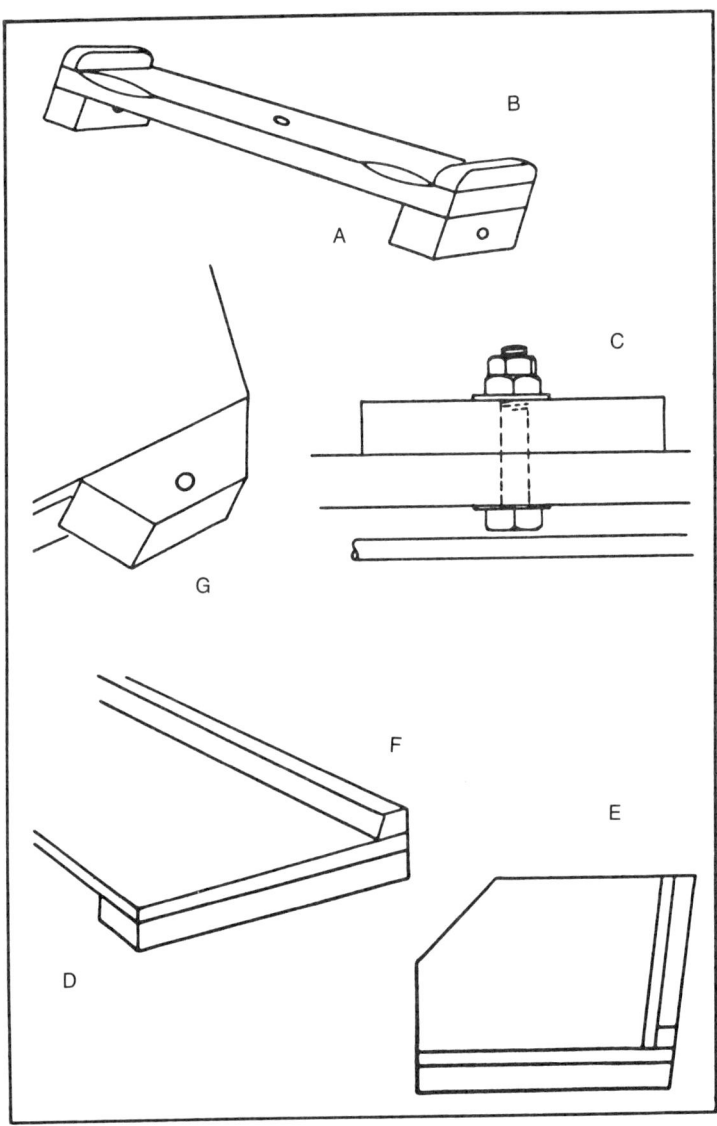

Fig. 7-3. Steering arrangements and seat construction of go-kart.

stiffeners across the ends (Fig. 7-2D). These are wide enough to take the rear bearing blocks and the seat sides.

The seat sides slope back slightly to increase comfort, and the front corners may be beveled or rounded (Fig. 7-3E). Bevel a stiffener across the seat to suit the slope of the back (Fig. 7-3F) and put stiffeners inside the ends, so the seat back is supported. Because the kart will be used outdoors and may be left out in wet weather, use exterior or marine plywood. Join the parts with waterproof glue and nails or screws.

When the kart is assembled, the chassis should be parallel with the ground or slope down to the front—not the other way. If you use pairs of wheels of different sizes, have the larger ones at the back. Arrange the axle height accordingly.

The rear bearings are fairly stout pieces of wood (Fig. 7-2D). Taper and drill them to match (Fig. 7-3G). Mount them under the seat sides.

Use glue and six 1½-inch-by-8-gauge screws to attach the seat to the chassis wood. This joint often has to take considerable strain, so make it secure. Check that the axle comes squarely across the chassis. If it is not square, the kart will tend to pull to one side.

Steering is by the feet. It helps to also have a loop of rope through holes in the footrest (Fig. 7-2E), so hands can help the feet when the truck is being pushed by someone else, or it is coasting down a slope. The rope loop is also useful for pulling the kart.

There are some possible modifications. One way of reducing the risk of wear on the front pivot bearing is to make the crosswise footrest in two pieces, with the chassis between. This can be based on the original design, with spacing pieces to a top bar (Fig. 7-4A). The axle will still come below through bearing blocks.

Some wheels can be mounted on stub axles or even long bolts. The axles can come between the crosswise parts (Fig. 7-4B) through the spacing blocks. This lowers the front, and the rear bearing blocks can also be shallower. Let the pieces be wide enough for the axles or bolts to go through and have a good hold. Otherwise, wear will occur soon in a short hole, so the wheels begin to wobble. If a nut cannot be used inside, drill through the axle for a split pin.

It is not difficult to adapt the seating so two children can use the kart, with one sitting backwards and pushing the kart with his feet on the ground. Make the seat with its back upright. Extend the bottom and sides to form another position (Fig. 7-4C). Have a longer chassis, so the double seat is supported by it.

Move the axle supports back. Otherwise, the weight of the rear child behind the original axle position may be enough to tilt the new rear edge (Fig. 7-4D).

Round all edges, particularly around the seat. Round well where the feet will come on the footrest. Ribbed rubber or other nonslip material can be put over these edges. Some padding in the set may

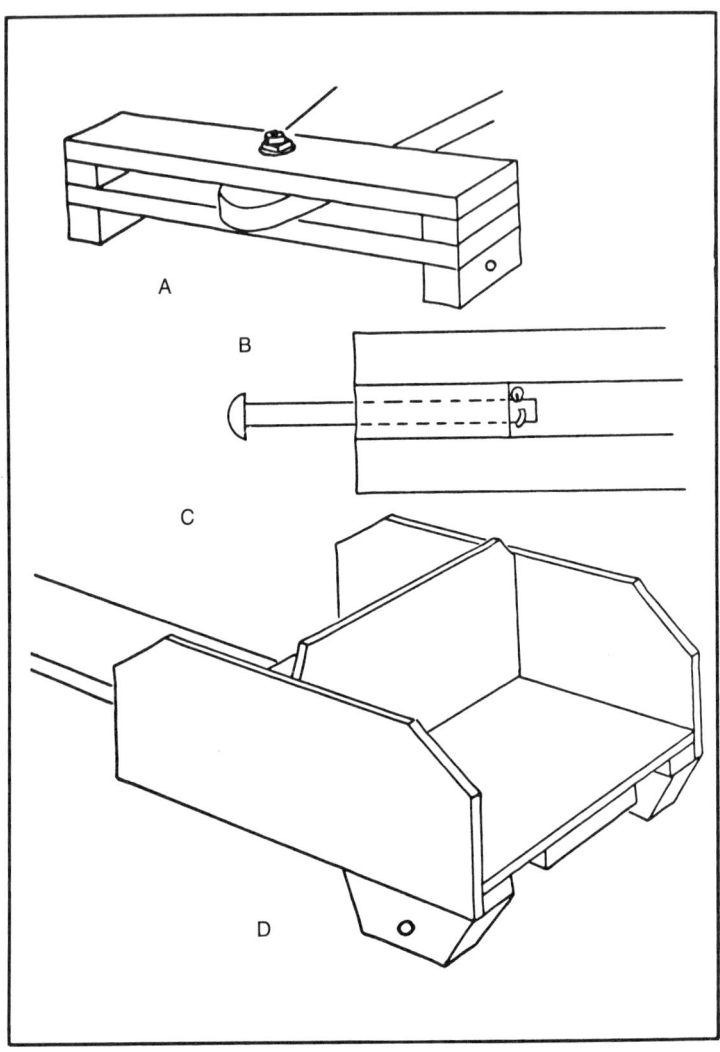

Fig. 7-4. Alternative steering and double seat for go-kart.

be appreciated, but do not have a loose cushion, which may slip just at the wrong moment.

If the wheels and axles are used ones, you can clean their bearing surfaces and repack them with grease. If they are to be repainted, remove greasy dirt with kerosene or a degreasing fluid first. Paint all the woodwork with bright colors, both for decoration and weatherproofing.

Materials List for Go-Kart

1 chassis	6 × 36 × 1
1 footrest	3 × 17 × 1
2 foot bearings	1½ × 3 × 1½
1 seat	10 × 16 × ½ plywood
2 seat sides	8 × 12 × ½ plywood
1 seat back	8 × 16 × ½ plywood
2 rear bearings	3 × 9 × 2
2 seat stiffeners	2 × 10 × 1
1 seat stiffener	¾ × 16 × ¾
2 back stiffeners	¾ × 9 × ¾

Project 8

Swing Set

A swing set and slide can give children hours of backyard fun. This all-wood structure is much more attractive than its commercial metal counterpart and, with proper finishing, is equally suited to an outdoor, permanent installation.

The size shown allows for two swings, or there is the alternative of a climbing frame or ladder in place of one swing (Fig. 8-1). If space is limited, the same construction can be used to make a narrower structure for just one swing.

The swing's framework gets its stability from inverted V-shaped legs, thrust into the ground. The slide also utilizes this wide stance for stability and should also be firmly planted in the ground with concrete footings.

Make the swing first. Cut the legs first, to get the proper angle for the top joints where legs meet crossbar. At the tops, notch the legs into the beam, but put the stiffening gussets inside and outside (Fig. 8-2A). If the legs are securely planted in the ground, the joints may prove strong enough. Strip metal brackets can be added as a further guard against movement (Fig. 8-2B). Shelf brackets may be adapted. They can be made from strips of ¼-inch by 1½-inch steel extending about 6 inches along each arm.

The swing(s) should be hung from ring bolts going through the beam. It is unwise to merely tie around the beam. Suitable bolts are ⅜-inch in diameter and long enough to go through a 4-inch thickness. Put a large washer under the nut to spread the load on

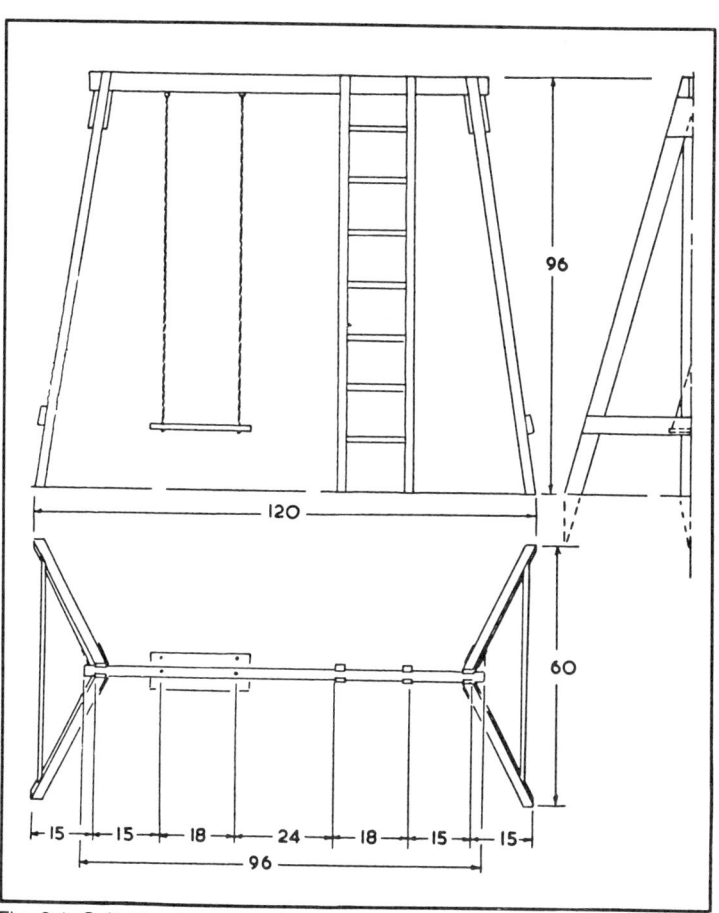

Fig. 8-1. Suitable sizes for swing and ladder.

the wood. For the strongest assembly, drill bolt holes for a very close fit. The bolt has to be driven through, so there is no risk of later movement.

The swing seat is a plain board (Fig. 8-2C). If it is thick waterproof plywood. it may need no other preparation. If the seat is solid wood, two battens underneath at the hole positions will prevent warping and strengthen the seat.

If synthetic rope is used, it will not suffer from exposure to the weather. Natural fiber rope has to be treated with preservative. Choose rope at least ½ inch in diameter, so a child can grip it easily. Ideally, the rope is spliced around a metal thimble at the ring bolt (Fig. 8-2D) and again spliced where the parts join above the seat

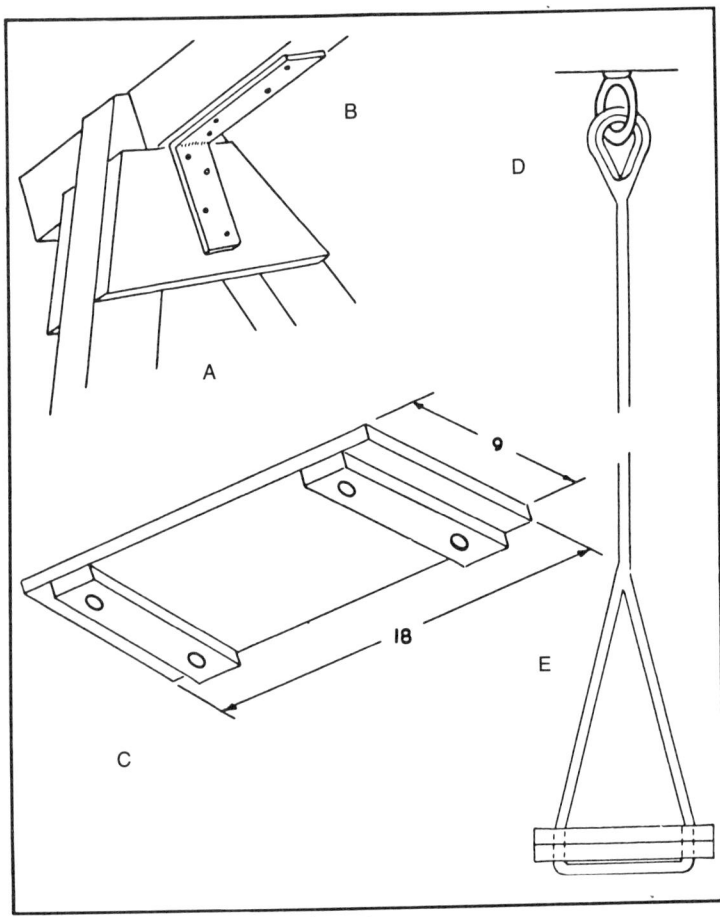

Fig. 8-2. Constructional details for swing.

(Fig. 8-2E). If you are unable to splice, knotting will be satisfactory although not so good looking. More information on splicing and knotting can be found in my book *Practical Knots & Ropework* (TAB Book No. 1237).

If a ladder is to be used instead of a second swing, notch the sides into the beam (Fig. 8-3A). This prevents movement and helps support the beam. Point the bottom to go into the ground. Mark out for the rungs to be equally spaced (Fig. 8-3B). Holes do not have to go right through. If you have the use of a drill press to make the holes squarely to the surfaces, the greatest accuracy comes from drilling right through both sides at the same time.

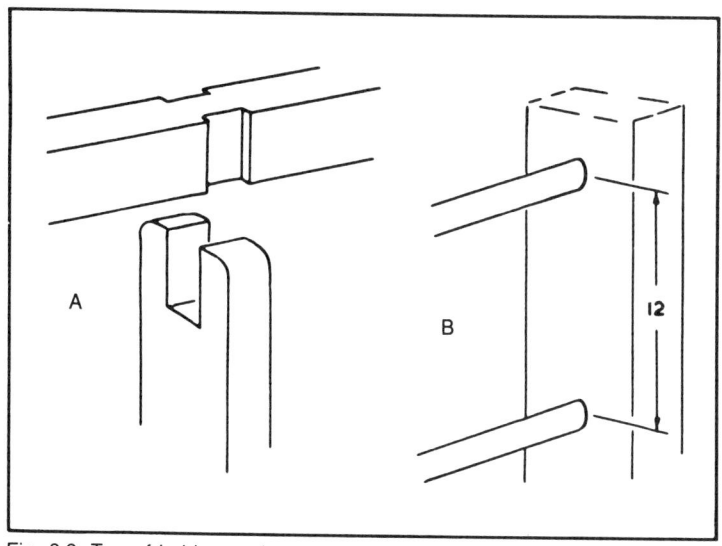

Fig. 8-3. Top of ladder, and rung spacing for swing.

Treat the wood with preservative. Assemble with rustproof nails or screws. As there are no permanent lengthwise pieces to hold the lower parts of the structure in shape, you may nail on some temporary crossbars to hold the shape until you have the legs firmly embedded in the ground.

SLIDE

This slide (Fig. 8-4) is best mounted with the upright parts set in concrete (Fig. 8-4A). If permanent installation in this manner is impossible, the legs can be cut at ground level, and wide feet are added (Fig. 8-4B) braced with plywood gussets. Treat the slide supports in a similar way. The slide should not be used completely freestanding. It is better to temporarily peg the feet to the ground or hold them down with weights like bags of sand.

Use wood planed all around and select straight pieces for the long posts and slide sides, as any twist or warp cannot be pulled out with connecting wood. Mark the heights and positions of other parts on the vertical posts. If you have sufficient floor space to set out a side view of the tower full-size, that helps in getting the positions of other parts. Otherwise, it is possible to lay down the marked vertical post and put the other pieces of wood that form a side in position so as to get their lengths, angles, and positions.

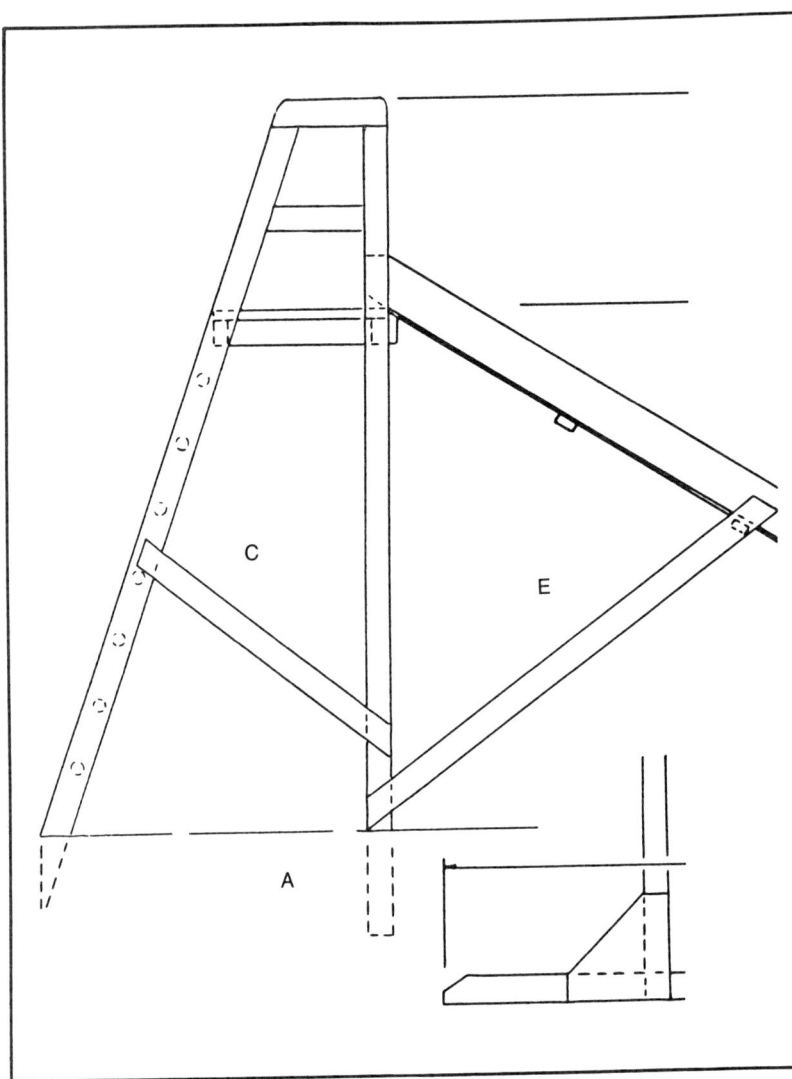

Fig. 8-4. Outdoor slide dimensions.

At the top, the platform rests on supports (Fig. 8-5A). The front one projects 1 inch and will also come under the slide (Fig. 8-5B). The tops are best joined with open mortise and tenon joints (Fig. 8-5C). The other parts are joined with plain mortise and tenons.

Mark out the ladder sides to give even step spacing between the floor and the platform top. Drill right through for the rungs and

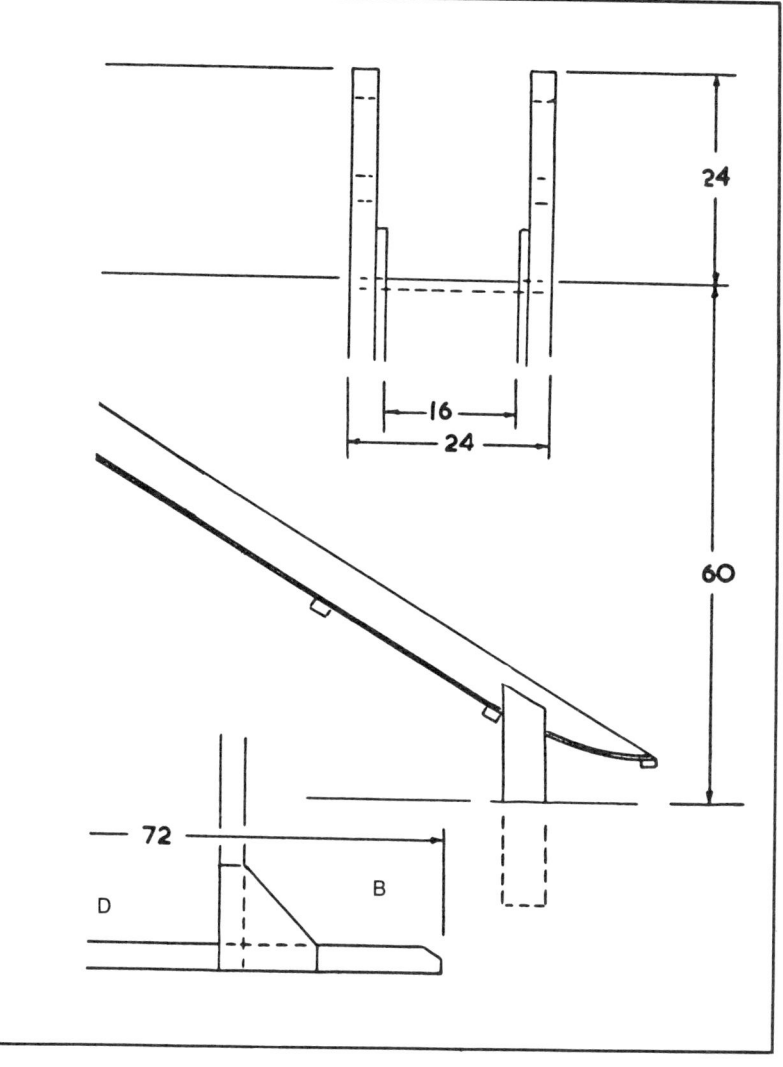

wedge them as you glue them in place (Fig. 8-5D). Put diagonal braces between the centers of the ladder sides and near the bottoms of the vertical posts (Fig. 8-4C).

If the posts are to go into concrete, soak the bottoms in a preservative. Mark what will be the ground level on them.

If there are to be feet, cut off the posts at ground level and tenon

Fig. 8-5. Tower details for outdoor slide.

them into the crosswise feet. Put plywood gussets on each side of the upright posts and on the underside of the sloping posts (Fig. 8-4D).

The platform can be a piece of thick waterproof plywood or manufactured board. The width can be made with several pieces of solid wood.

The slide show is drawn at 30 degrees to horizontal. The exact angle is not critical, although making it too steep will bring the child down too fast. A very shallow slope may not be sufficiently exciting.

At the top, the sides are screwed inside the upright posts (Fig. 8-6A). Round these ends thoroughly, so there is nothing rough where a child is lowering himself or herself onto the slide. At the bottom, cut the ends of the sides to a long sweeping curve. The amount of curve depends on the plywood used. Try bending the plywood and draw that curve (Fig. 8-6B). The curve is intended to let the user swing outwards and land on his or her feet.

The length of the slide is more that the length of the common 8-foot plywood sheet. Longer plywood is obtainable, but it does not

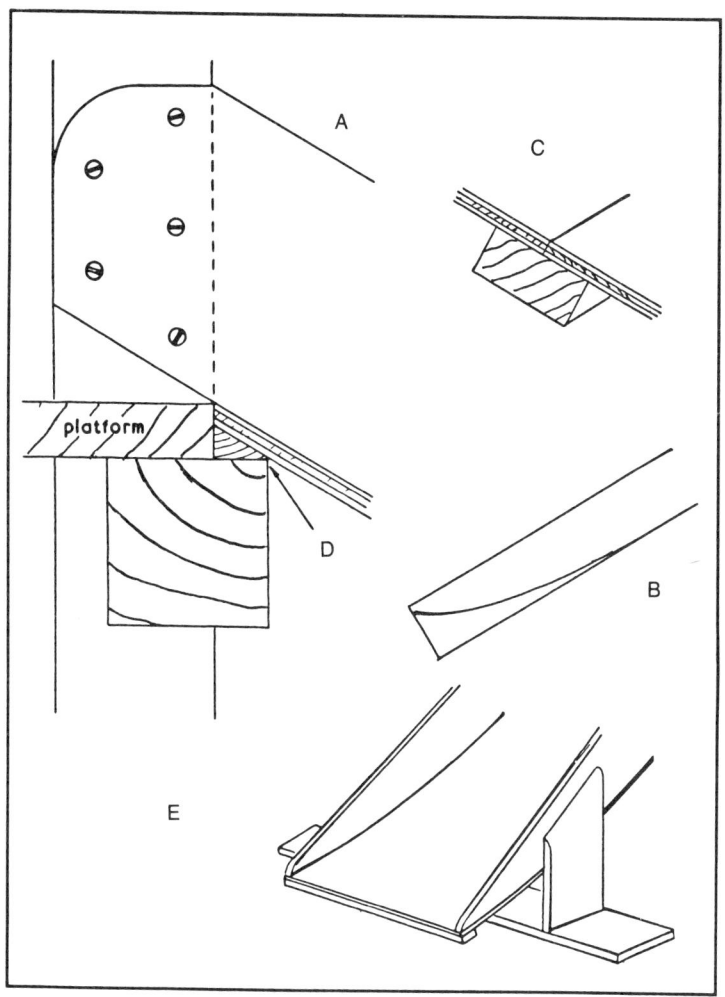

Fig. 8-6. Assembly details for slide.

matter if you have to join two pieces. Let the long piece extend up from the bottom, so the joint comes on a flat part. Glue and screw the plywood under the sides. Put stiffeners across at intervals, arranging one under the plywood joint (Fig. 8-6C) if there is one. The number of stiffeners needed depends on the inherent stiffness of the plywood. Arrange one at the bottom of the slide.

Where the slide meets the platform, pack up the extending edge of the platform support (Fig. 8-6D). Blend platform and slide edges by rounding them slightly, if necessary.

Arrange diagonal braces from near the center of the slide to the vertical posts (Fig. 8-4E). Do not take the brace ends to the edges of the slide sides. Cut them back and round them, so they are clear of hands sliding on the sides.

At the bottom, attach supports on each side to keep the end of the slide about 6 inches off the ground. Allow enough length for setting into the ground, or cut off the supports and join them to crosswise feet (Fig. 8-6E). As with the braces, keep the tops of the supports clear of sliding hands.

Materials List for Swing and Slide

Swing
1 beam	$4 \times 96 \times 2$
4 legs	$4 \times 120 \times 2$
2 braces	$4 \times 60 \times 2$
4 gussets	$9 \times 16 \times 1$
1 swing seat	$9 \times 24 \times ¾$
2 ladder sides	$4 \times 110 \times 2$
7 ladder rungs	$1¼ \times 18$ round rod

Slide
4 posts	$3 \times 110 \times 3$
2 tops	$3 \times 18 \times 3$
1 platform support	$3 \times 24 \times 3$
3 platform supports	$3 \times 24 \times 2$
2 rails	$3 \times 18 \times 2$
1 platform	$24 \times 24 \times 1$
7 rungs	1×24 round rod
2 slide sides	$5 \times 130 \times 1$
5 slide stiffeners	$2 \times 19 \times 1$
1 slide	$19 \times 125 \times ⅜$ plywood
2 braces	$3 \times 65 \times 1$
2 slide supports	$6 \times 28 \times 1$
2 feet (optional)	$3 \times 72 \times 3$
2 feet (optional)	$6 \times 36 \times 1$
6 gussets (optional)	$9 \times 9 \times ½$ plywood
2 braces	$3 \times 42 \times 1$

Project 9

Rocking Chair

Swingers of a more sedate variety will appreciate this cushioned rocker (Fig. 9-1). The construction is simple enough for the average woodworker, while the variety of joints and upholstery techniques broaden skills in preparation for more exciting projects to come.

You can use either elastic webbing to support the cushions or adjust the framing to fit standard size coil springs. The method of support must be chosen before starting on the woodwork. For rubber webbing, there are metal fittings to squeeze on to cut ends (Fig. 9-2A). A nail or screw can go through the fitting, or a common way of attachment uses an angled plowed groove (Fig. 9-2B). A coil spring will hook on to a nail or screw in a rabbet (Fig. 9-2C) or a groove (Fig. 9-2D). It is also possible to get metal strips to screw to the wood and take the springs at intervals (Fig. 9-2E).

Start by making the seat frame. The webbing or springs will fit crosswise. Prepare the side pieces to suit the chosen type.

Corner joints can be dovetails (See Project 10) or bridles (Fig. 9-3A and B). See that the assembly is square. If there are doubts about its rigidity, put triangular blocks low down in the corners (Fig. 9-3C). When springs or webbing are fitted, space them at about 5-inch centers.

The front legs cross at right angles. Both parts are notched. The joints are screwed from inside and glued (Fig. 9-3D). The rear legs are notched to the same depth so front and back legs are in line.

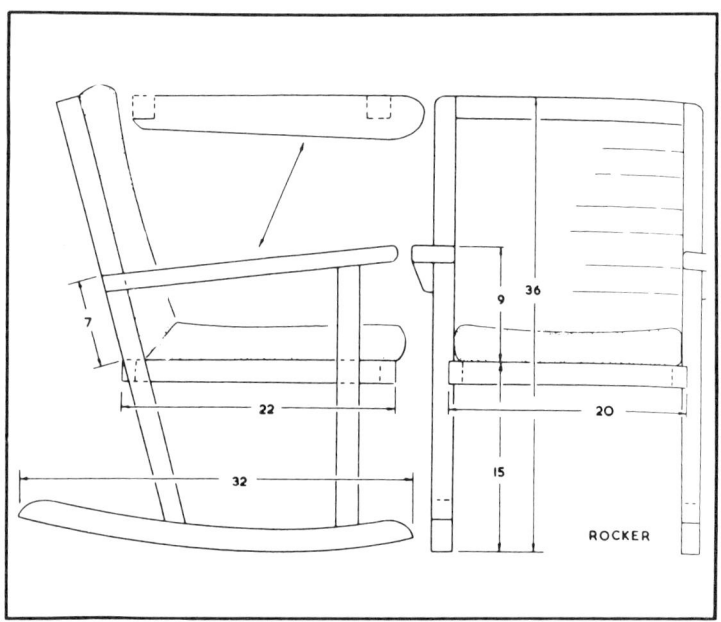

Fig. 9-1. Cushioned rocking chair of simple proportions.

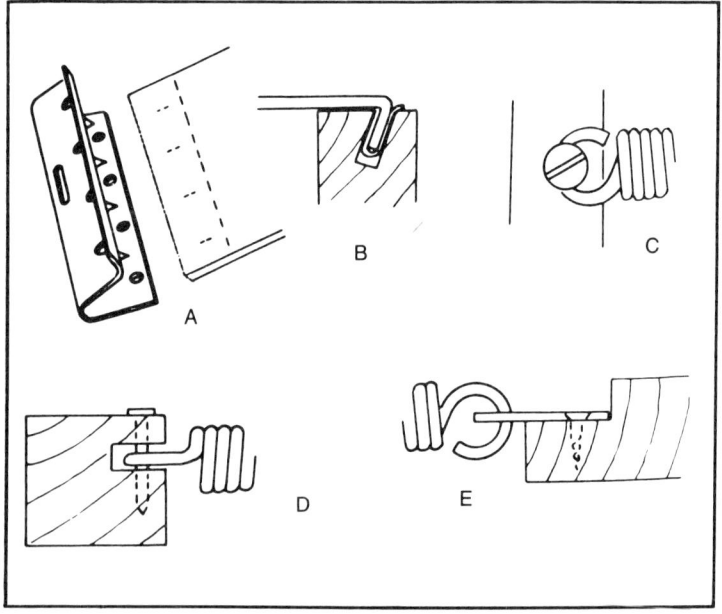

Fig. 9-2. Methods of attaching rubber webbing (A, B) or coil springs (C, D, E).

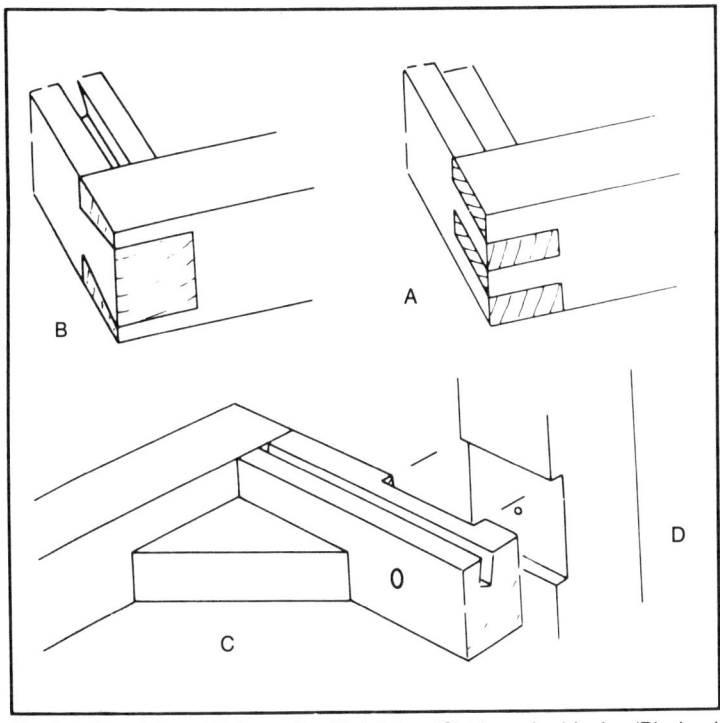

Fig. 9-3. Seat joints: (A) dovetails; (B) bridles; (C) triangular blocks; (D) glued joints fastened with screws.

Mark out the back legs with some extra left at the bottoms. Prepare the parts that come behind the cushion to take webbing or springs. Joints to the crossbar forming the top can be the same as in the corners of the seat. The back is drawn at 15 degrees to vertical. Mark the joint to the seat at this angle.

The arms tenon into the back leg (Fig. 9-4A) with a shallow notch at the outside. If an exposed joint is preferred at the front, use a similar arrangement there (Fig. 9-4B). Otherwise, use double tenons with fox wedging (Fig. 9-4C).

The rockers are cut from solid wood (Fig. 9-5A). A curve can be drawn using a long piece of wood and an awl as a compass. The best rocker curve is not quite part of the circumference of a circle. It is better if the curve flattens toward the extended rear end. It can be drawn around a sprung lath that is manipulated in the hands to get the required shape (Fig. 9-5B). When the chair is at rest, it should be resting on the part of the curve just behind the halfway

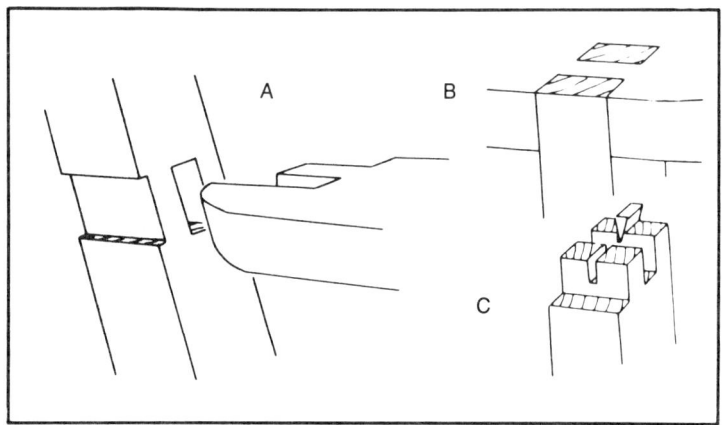

Fig. 9-4. Arm joints: (A) tenon; (B) exposed joint; (C) fox wedging.

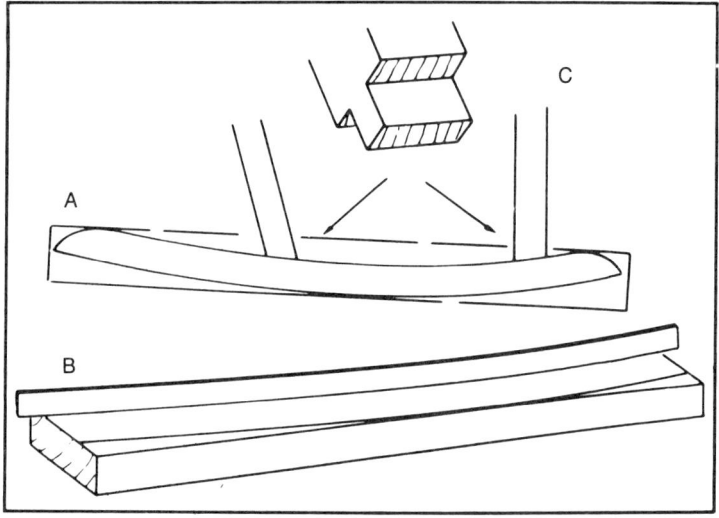

Fig. 9-5. Rocker (A) shapes and joints (B, C).

mark between the legs. The seat should then be slightly lower at the back than the front.

With a temporary assembly of one side, position a rocker over its legs and mark both legs and rocker with each other's positions. Use these marks as guides for marking and cutting the mortise and tenon joints (Fig. 9-5C). Do not weaken the rockers by cutting deep mortises.

Take off all sharp edges and round the outer corners. In particular, thoroughly round the parts of the arms that project

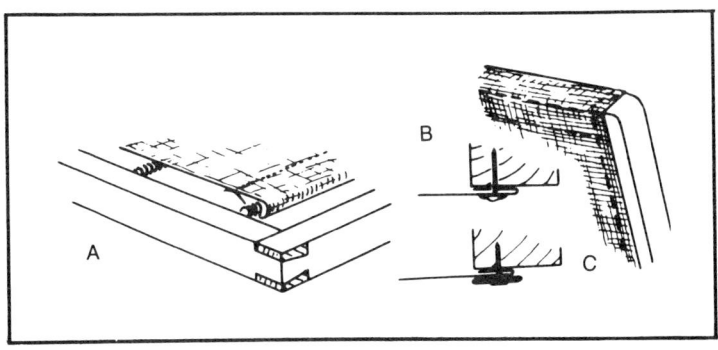

Fig. 9-6. Covering springs (A) and back (B, C).

forward. Check for squareness, or cushions will not fit evenly.

The cushions are rectangular pieces of 3-inch thick foam. They can be suitable stock cushions, or they can be made by sewing the covering inside out for all but the last seam at a narrow end. With the cover turned the right way and the foam pad pushed in, the last edge has to be sewn from outside. It is best to arrange for this to come where the cushions meet and it will not show.

Cushions can rest directly against webbing, but with springs it is better to put light, flexible cloth between them and the cushions. This can be tacked to the frame or it can be sewn around the end springs (Fig. 9-6A). The underside of the seat will not be seen, but the reverse side of the back will be covered with a piece of cloth. Use either a plain piece or one that matches the cushions. It would then be wrapped over the top and tacked to the frame (Fig. 9-6B). Use ornamental nails or thin nails through gimp (Fig. 9-6C).

Materials List for Rocker

2 front legs	$1\frac{1}{4} \times 25 \times 1\frac{3}{4}$
2 back legs	$1\frac{3}{4} \times 38 \times 1\frac{3}{4}$
2 seat frames	$1\frac{3}{4} \times 23 \times 1\frac{1}{4}$
2 seat frames	$1\frac{3}{4} \times 21 \times 1\frac{1}{4}$
1 top	$1\frac{3}{4} \times 24 \times 1\frac{3}{4}$
2 arms	$3\frac{1}{2} \times 25 \times 1\frac{1}{4}$
2 rockers	$5 \times 33 \times 1\frac{3}{4}$

Project 10

Dovetail Joints

Probably more than any other joints, dovetails are the cabinetmaker's joints. The dovetail form gives a joint that is secure in one direction without dependence on glue. A series of dovetails will lock two broad boards together so that they expand and contract together to prevent warping. Dovetails can be made so that they are not visible in one or both directions, and it is possible to examine a piece of furniture without knowing there are dovetails between parts. Exposed dovetails are regarded as design features in some furniture. There is nothing to equal dovetails for joining drawer sides to the front, and some connoisseurs pull out a drawer to see its side joints as an important point in assessing the quality of a piece of furniture.

The angled parts of a dovetail joint are usually called *tails* because they are like the tail of a dove. The projections on the other part that go between the tails are *pins*. The construction is seen in a single, through dovetail (Fig. 10-1A). In general carcase work, several dovetails are arranged across the joint (Fig. 10-1B). There are no recognized rules about the spacing of the parts of the joint or the number of parts to be used or their relative width. Individual cabinetmakers have their own ideas, and a beginner can discover customary arrangements by examining good furniture. The tails and pins have to be spaced across the wood and arithmetical considerations will settle exact sizes. In general, very wide tails should be avoided. Making them a little wider than the thickness of the wood is often satisfactory.

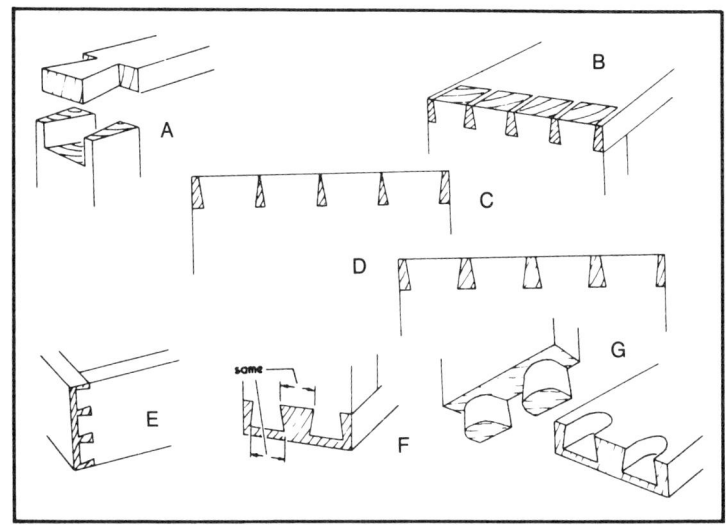

Fig. 10-1. Dovetails can be single (A) or multiple (B) and with pins wide (C) or narrow (D). A stopped dovetail (E) is hidden in one direction. Machine-made dovetails have tails and pins of the same width (F, G).

There was a time at the height of the handmade furniture period when cabinetmakers took a pride in making the pins very narrow (Fig. 10-1C). This might have shown their skill in cutting joints and the joints appear to have held together well, but there is more strength in wider pins. In reproduction work, it may be necessary to make joints with the narrowest possible pins. Otherwise, it is stronger and easier to give them a moderate width (Fig. 10-1D).

There are many places, like a drawer front, where the dovetail has to be partially hidden. This is a *half blind, stopped,* or *lap* dovetail joint (Fig. 10-1E). Details are the same as for a through joint. A part covers the ends of the dovetails. Most dovetail joints have to be made by hand, but there is a way to make this type of joint by machine. Machined joints can be identified by checking widths. The tails and pins will be found to be the same (Fig. 10-1F). Inside the joint the parts are rounded (Fig. 10-1G). It is possible to make such a joint with a template that clamps to the wood and acts as a guide to a cutter mounted in an electric drill. The result is quite satisfactory, but it would not really be classed as fine cabinetwork. In good quality work, it is better to make the joints by hand and arrange the pin widths to be narrower than the tails.

The slope of the side of a dovetail has to be enough to prevent it from pulling back, yet not so much that its tip cuts across short lines of grain that might break off. In soft woods, a slightly wider angle is needed than would be satisfactory in harder woods. However, the difference is slight. The angle should be between 1 in 6 and 1 in 9. For soft woods, a slope of 1 in 7 can be used (Fig. 10-2A). For hardwoods 1 in 8 is better (Fig. 10-2B). Uniformity of slope is essential for the sake of appearance. An adjustable bevel can be set to the slope after laying out the angle on the edge of a board (Fig. 10-2C). A piece of sheet metal can be bent and used as a template (Fig. 10-2D) or a similar thing can be made from wood (Fig. 10-2E). A more elaborate tool, if much dovetailing is to be done, has a blade with softwood and hardwood angles on opposite sides.

When laying out dovetails, allow for having to remove the waste between them with a bevel-edged chisel. Make sure that the gaps are somewhat wider at their bottoms than the chisel you intend to use. It is common for there to be pins at the edges of the joint (Fig. 10-3A), but in some situations it is better to have half dovetails outside (Fig. 10-3B). This is satisfactory, but if there is no particular need for it, choose the other arrangement. Dovetails do not have to be all the same widths, and some craftsmen mark them out by eye. In any position that will show, they should be uniformly arranged. Some traditional cabinetmakers used one narrower tail near an unsupported edge (Fig. 10-3C) where it might be considered to

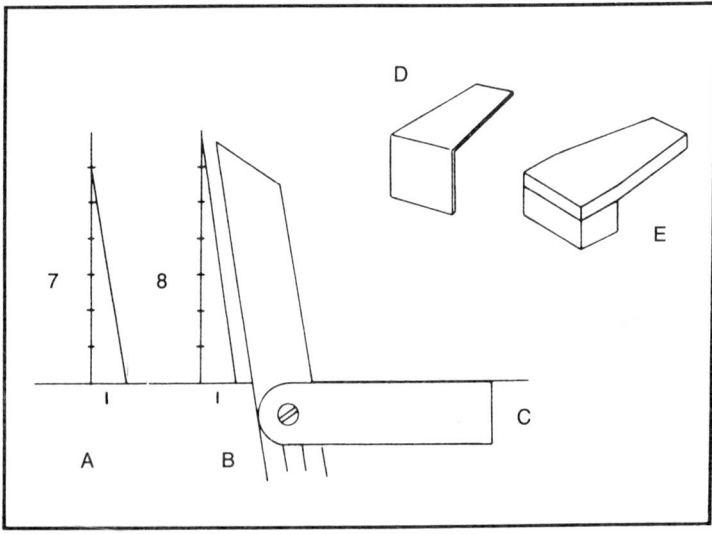

Fig. 10-2. Dovetail angles are slightly wider in softwoods than hardwoods (A, B, C). Simple gauges can take the place of an adjustable bevel. Wood or metal templates (D, E) can be used.

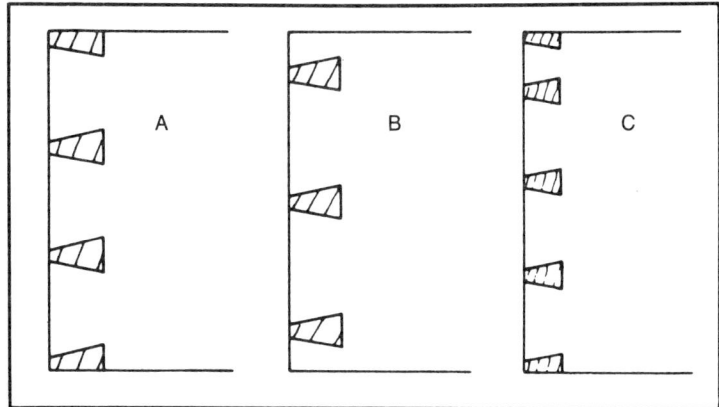

Fig. 10-3. Pins (A) or dovetails (B) can come outside and sometimes a smaller tail is used at the top of an open box (C).

provide a little extra strength. This also allows him to make up for taking less trouble in spacing the main tails.

MAKING THROUGH DOVETAIL JOINTS

Dovetail joints can be marked out and cut with the tails first or the pins first. For an ordinary through dovetail joint, it does not matter which way is chosen. The ends of the wood should be planed square to the face sides and edges, but they can be just slightly too long. If much excess length is left, the gaps between tail ends will get closer and removing the waste becomes difficult.

If the tails are to be cut first, mark the width of the other piece back from the end. Leave just a little excess for planing after assembly. Do this with pencil and square it around all four faces. Space the tails and mark them with pencil (Fig. 10-4A). If two parts, such as the opposite sides of a box have to match, mark the tails on one piece. Then square across the two while they are clamped or held in a vise (Fig. 10-4B). Saw down the sides of the tails with a fine backsaw. Keep the kerfs on the waste side of the line and watch the cut at the far side as well as at the front to see that it does not go below the line. Two or even four pieces can be sawn at one time.

Turn the wood on edge and cut each side. For the cleanest ends, go over the pencil line at each place with a knife to sever the fibers before sawing. Have each piece supported on a flat piece of scrap wood on the bench top while chopping out the waste between the tails. Cut about halfway from each side to avoid breaking out. Be

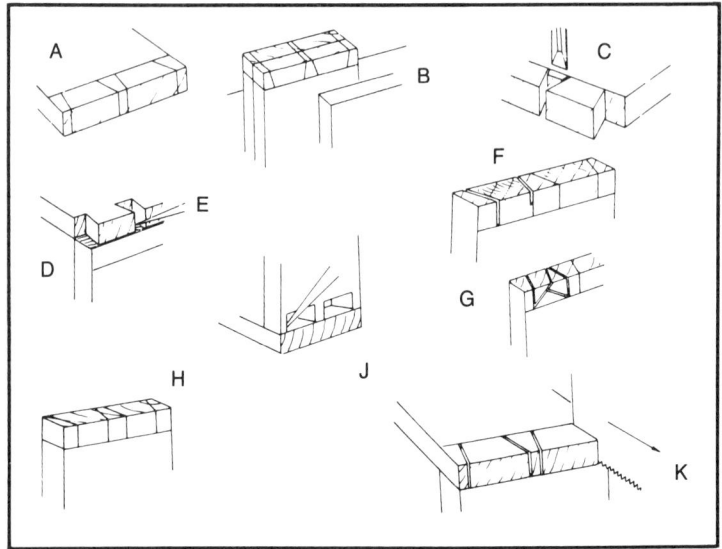

Fig. 10-4. Tails can be cut first and used to mark the pins (A, B, C). Alternatively, mark the tails from the pins (E, F, G). Another way is to mark through saw cuts (H, J, K).

careful that the chisel is not levered against the ends of the pins where it would either damage them or break them off. Clear the waste by chopping from each side to within a short distance of the line. Then pare by hand back to the line (Fig. 10-4C). Check in each space to be sure that the cut goes right through straight and just touches the lines at each side. A lump in the middle or fibers still clinging in an angle will prevent close assembly. A very slight hollow is preferable to a lump.

Although matching parts can be sawn together, it is unlikely that they will finish so uniform as to be interchangeable. From this stage, mark each mating tail and pin part with numbers inside or some other means so that corners do not become mixed.

Have the thickness of the dovetail part, plus a little extra for planing, marked all round the part that will have the pins. Support the tail part over it (Fig. 10-4D). Use a fine steel point or a finely sharpened pencil to mark the outline of each tail (Fig. 10-4E). Use a try square to draw down to the line at each mark. The marked lines indicate the actual sizes of the tails. To get a close fit, the kerfs must be kept on the waste side of the lines (Fig. 10-4F). For a first attempt, it is advisable to scribble with pencil on the waste parts as a guard against sawing on the wrong side of a line.

The waste can be chopped out, but it is possible to remove some of it by sawing diagonally (Fig. 10-4G). Work back to the lines by chopping from each side. Remember to taper in the width when chopping from the wider side. Tilt the chisel to avoid damaging the far side of a pin. Then carefully pare back to the line on each side with a wider chisel than was used for chopping out.

If the pins are to be made first, space the tail outlines across the end and square down to the thickness line (Fig. 10-4H). Cut away the sockets between the pins in the way just described. Stand the pin part in position on the piece for the dovetails and mark the shapes (Fig. 10-4J). One advantage of this method is that there is more room for using a spike or pencil. Square across the ends of the wood and cut the tails on the waste side of the lines.

Another way of marking the pins from the dovetailed part is to saw the sides of the tails. Do not chop out the waste. Put the wood in position on the other piece and draw the end of the saw back in each kerf a few times to mark the end grain (Fig. 10-4K). Remove the top piece and finish it by cutting between the tails. The mark made by the saw does not allow for the thickness of the cut. Do not continue to saw in the positions marked. Instead, relocate the saw for each cut on the waste side of that initial shallow kerf. Otherwise the joint will finish loose by the thickness of the saw cut at each place.

A skilled craftsman depends on his ability to work accurately and does not make a trial assembly of a dovetail joint. As with mortise and tenon and other joints, a trial assembly might cause wear at the edges of a joint and there will be a better fit if the first assembly is the last. If you want to try a joint together, enter the tails only partly into their sockets so that you can see if they are correct. Do not push the parts tightly together yet.

In the final glued assembly of a wide joint, be careful to avoid local pressure that might cause cracking or difficulty elsewhere. Make sure that all tails are entered in their sockets. Then spread pressure with a strip of wood across and clamp over that at both ends or use a mallet or hammer over it. Most of these joints have to finish at right angles, so check squareness before allowing the glue to set. If it is a four-sided assembly with dovetail joints at the corners, check squareness by measuring diagonals.

MAKING LAP DOVETAIL JOINTS

The half-blind or lap dovetail joint is particularly associated with joining drawer sides to the front, but there are many other uses for it. In effect, it is the same as a through dovetail joint with a piece behind the pins covering the ends of the tails. Usually that part is thicker than the other to allow for it. The overlapping piece should not be too thin, although it looks neater if kept to a minimum. The sockets for the tails have to be chopped towards it, and a very thin part might crack or allow the chisel to break through. For the usual cabinet drawer, allow about 3/16 of an inch.

The dovetailed part is similar to that of a through dovetail joint. However, it must be exactly the proper length because this joint does not allow for planing the ends later. Mark on each piece how much the other will overlap (Fig. 10-5A).

If the dovetailed part is to be made first, mark it out and cut it in the same way as for a through dovetail joint. Put it in position against the line on the other part and mark the shapes of the tails (Fig. 10-5B). Square down to the line (Fig. 10-5C). Saw diagonally on the waste side of the line at each position (Fig. 10-5D). A small amount of waste can be removed with the saw (Fig. 10-5E), but the rest of the waste will have to be cut out with a chisel.

Have the wood flat on a piece of scrap wood on the bench top (preferably held with a holdfast). Chop away diagonally first (Fig. 10-5F). Make other cuts first across the fibers (Fig. 10-5G), then pare towards these cuts (Fig. 10-5H). Do this a little at a time, with

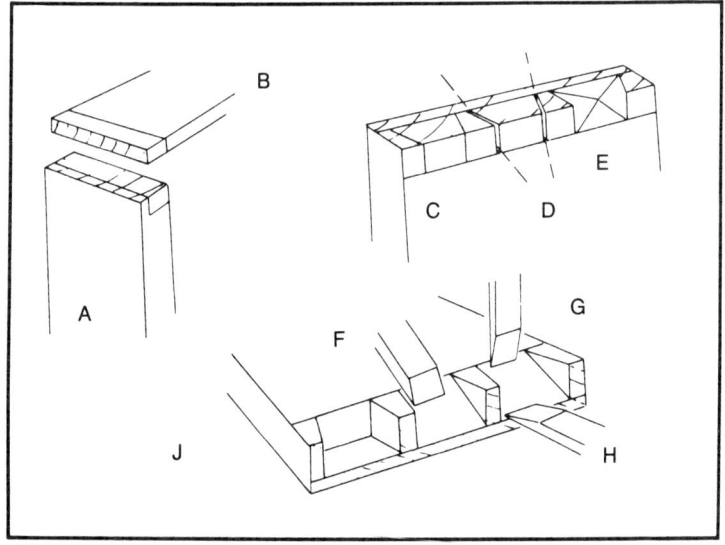

Fig. 10-5. A stopped dovetail (A, B, C, D, E) involves more work with chisels (F, G, H, J).

the cross grain cut always ahead of the paring along with grain, until the socket is to shape (Fig. 10-5J) and there are fibers left in the angles. It might be possible to remove some of the waste by drilling or a router cutter could be used. Great care is needed to avoid going too far. When chopping or paring, be very careful not to break through the thin covering part.

The pins could be marked and cut first if you prefer to work that way. Carefully position the wood on the part for the tails at the exact limit when you are marking on the end grain.

For a drawer, the bottom will fit into a groove at the front and into each side. The lap dovetail joint has to be arranged to enclose this so that the groove is not visible outside. The groove could be in the bottom tail in a normal arrangement, but to get it lower it is better to use a half tail at the bottom (Fig. 10-6A) with the groove through it meeting that across the front.

At the back of a drawer, it is common for the bottom to go through with the back above it, usually held to the sides with through dovetails (Fig. 10-6B). If the drawer slides on runners there will be a piece to increase the bearing surface on each side (Fig. 10-6C).

HIDDEN DOVETAILS

The next step after the lap dovetail joint is one where the details of the joint are hidden in both directions. This is a *stopped lap* or *blind lap* dovetail joint. The pins and tails meet normally, but both

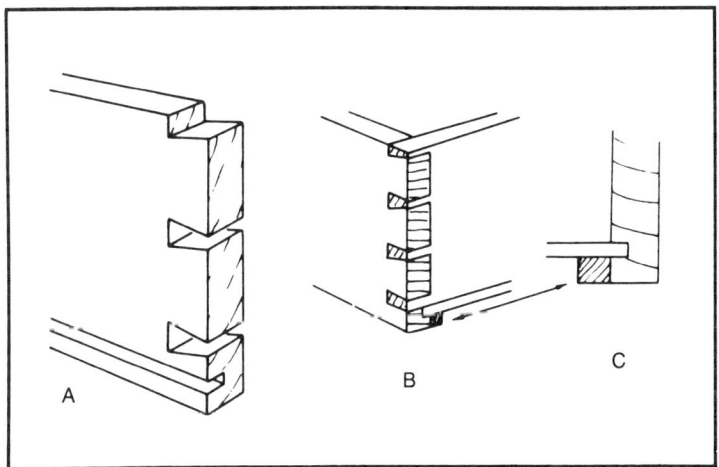

Fig. 10-6. In a drawer, the groove for the bottom can be hidden in the front bottom tail (A) and taken under the back (B, C).

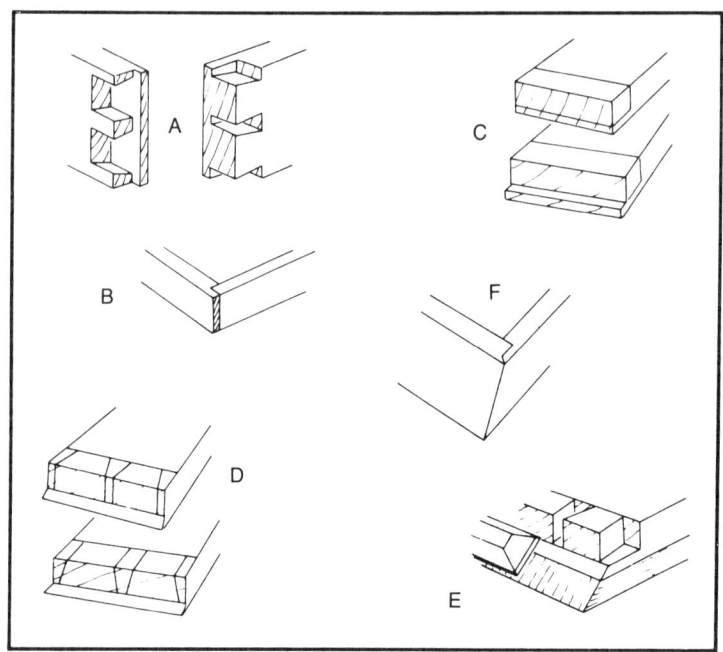

Fig. 10-7. Dovetails (A, B) can be hidden by parts cut (C) outside, either squarely or mitered (D, E, F).

parts have extra thickness outside to cover them (Fig. 10-7A). When the joint is closed, only one overlap is visible (Fig. 10-7B).

Mark both pieces with the amount they overlap and cut back one piece by the covering part (Fig. 10-7C). Mark one part and cut it out. A small amount of sawing can be done on the part without the overhang, but most cutting of both parts will have to be with chisels. Mark the second part from the first. If the actual joint is visualized as a through dovetail joint and the outer parts are considered as additions, the steps in cutting the joint will be understood.

That joint assembles with a narrow piece of end visible in one direction, but it can be eliminated by altering it to a "housed and mitered dovetail joint." Both pieces are given extensions which meet in a mitered corner (Fig. 10-7D). The extensions have to be pared carefully so that they will meet throughout their length when the joint is pulled tight. A safe way to do this accurately is to clamp a thick piece of wood that is planed to 45 degrees below the dovetail and use this as a guide for a wide chisel (Fig. 10-7E).

When that joint is closed, the outer corner will be a tight miter. At the edges, part of the form of the joint can be seen (Fig. 10-7F).

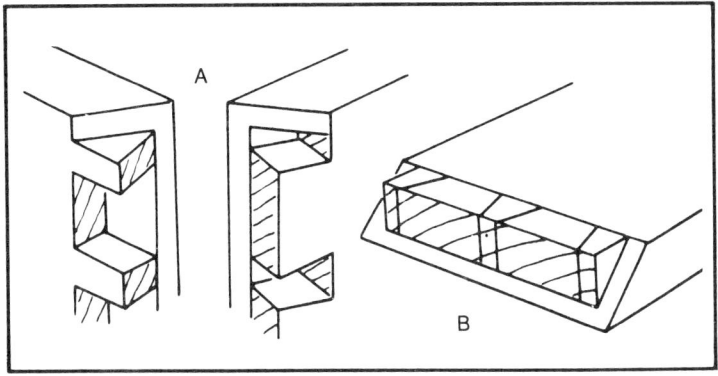

Fig. 10-8. In a fully hidden mitered dovetail (A), there are miters at the ends (B) of the joint.

For many purposes, this does not matter. If the edge is also to appear as a miter, it is necessary to make the joint into a *secret dovetail* or *blind dovetail* joint.

The secret version is best visualized as the *housed and metered* joint, with extra thickness top and bottom. It is mitered (Fig. 10-8A). Mark out the parts that will make the joint as for a through dovetail joint. Extra thickness goes outside each part for the corner miter and more is needed to continue this miter at the edges (Fig. 10-8B).

After cutting back for the corner mitered parts, it might be best to cut the edge miters so that what is left can be marked out for the tails and pins. Leave cutting the main part of the long miter until the sockets have been cut. You will almost certainly cut into the extension pieces at some stage, but this will not matter if there is still some surplus wood there. Very little of the joint can be sawn and it is mostly careful work with chisels

Project 11

Dovetailed Chest

The dovetail method of construction given in the previous project has traditionally been used for small storage boxes and chests. This chest has its lid framing as a continuation of the body of the box (Fig. 11-1A). This is a method frequently used today, but none of the earlier larger chests appear to have used the technique. The advantage of making a box this way is that the lid will always match the box.

In the example, the joint line is marked with a space to allow for the saw kerf and dovetails arranged each side of it (Fig. 11-1B). Joints are cut and the sides and ends of the box glued together. Top and bottom are fixed—in this case with glue and nails—and both can overlap slightly, to be planed off later. The top of this box is planed to a curve before fixing (Fig. 11-1C).

The outside of the box is cleaned up all round, with excess wood planed level and the surfaces smoothed, except for final sanding. The lid is not cut off until this stage. The original makers cut around between the lines with a hand saw, but if a table saw is available, it is a simple matter to set the fence and go around the four faces. Unless it is obvious from grain markings, it may be advisable to mark the mating parts of lid and box, so they are put back together the right way.

The sawn edges have to be planed level and any surplus glue inside the box cleaned away. Two hinges are arranged at the back. There is no need for any sort of handle, but some of these boxes were given small turned knobs on the front of the lid and matching turned feet under the corners of the box (Fig. 11-1D).

A variation on this is made in the same way, except the top and bottom are allowed to project all round, then given molded edges (Fig. 11-1E). The back could be cut level so the lid would open some way, but if the lid projected there it could be arranged to act as a stop when the lid was vertical (Fig. 11-1F). Either box could be lined with velvet to make a jewelry case.

One way of avoiding the use of hinges, yet provide a secure lid instead of having it lift off, was to extend the ends of the box at least as high as the thickness of the lid. Sometimes the ends reached high enough to be fretted to form decorative handles (Fig. 11-1G). The lid fitted over the sides, but between the ends. The underside of its back edge was rounded and pivots were provided by nails through the ends (Fig. 11-1H).

A sliding lid was another secure type. This was seen in school children's pencil boxes, but the idea was also used in boxes for other purposes. In the simplest form, the sides of the box were grooved and the lid shaped to slide in the grooves. Simplest was a V-cut (Fig. 11-1J), but a stronger lid edge comes from plowing a groove and beveling its top edge (Fig. 11-1K). In a simple box the end overlaps the sides and provides a stop for the lid, which passes over the other end and is either given a knob or a finger notch (Fig. 11-1L).

In a better box, the lid also enters a groove in the end. To avoid marring the surface where a groove in the overlapping parts ran through, the top corners should be mitered for the depth of the grooves (Fig. 11-1M). This can be done whether the box has overlapped nailed corners or dovetail joints.

Materials List for Dovetailed Chest

2 Ends	$6 \times 5 \times \frac{1}{2}$
1 Top	$5 \times 8 \times 1$
2 Sides	$6 \times 8 \times \frac{1}{2}$
1 Bottom	$5 \times 8 \times \frac{1}{2}$

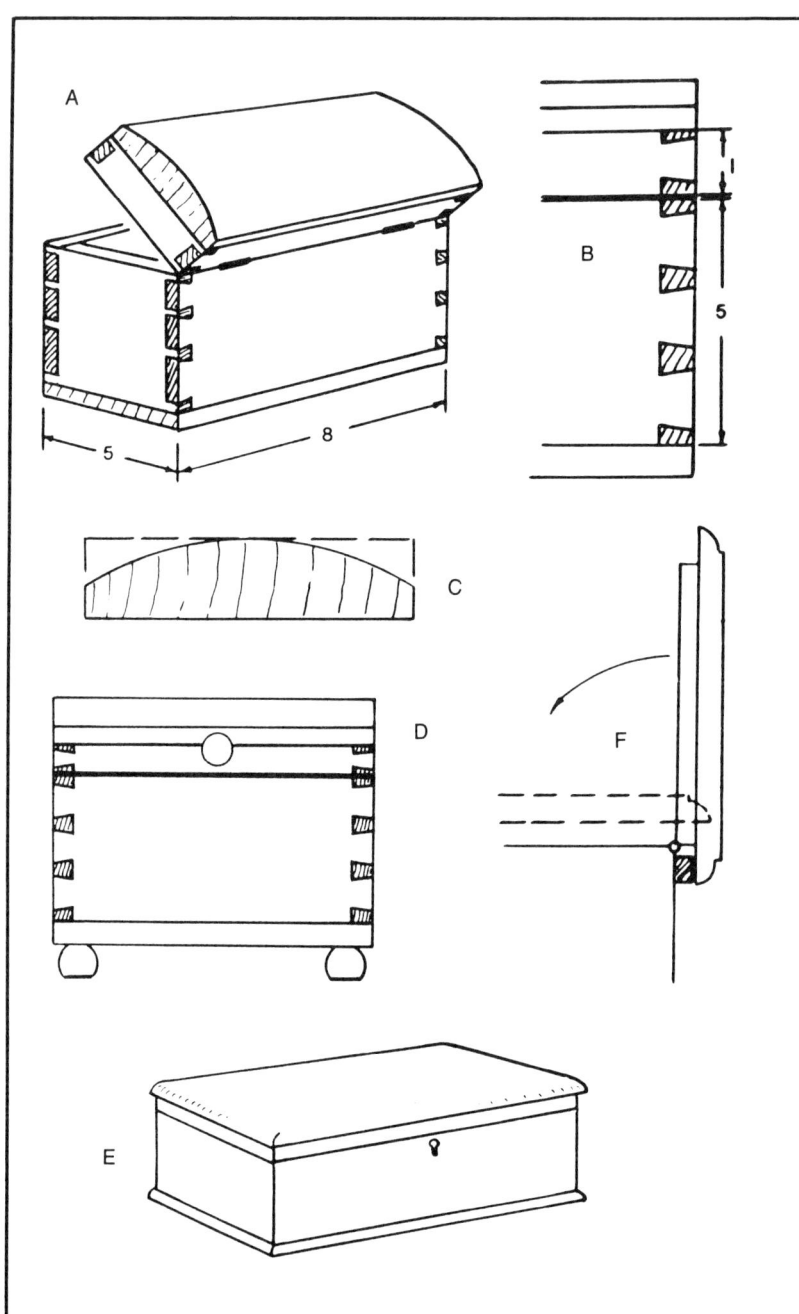

Fig. 11-1. Dovetailed chest features various lid options.

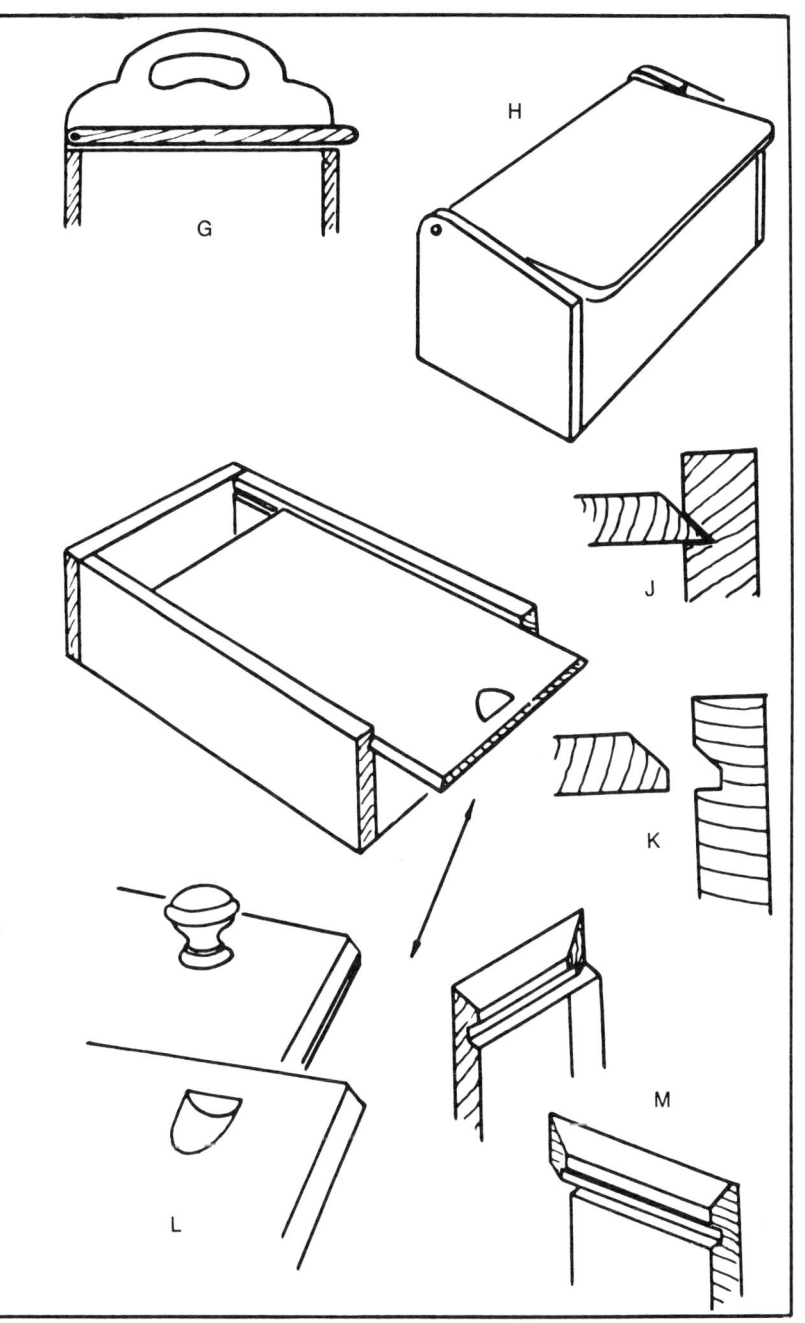

Project 12

Lathe Turning

Fancy legs, chair rails, and round objects are produced with handheld tools on a lathe. It is a hand process more than a mechanical one, and there is plenty of scope for a craftsman to show his skill.

A lathe need not be very complicated and for most purposes it is better for being simple. The important part is the headstock (Fig. 12-1A) where a shaft takes its drive from a motor. Its bearings should be as free of vibrations as possible. At one or both ends, the shaft is threaded to take fittings that drive the wood.

The headstock is mounted on the bed (Fig. 12-1B). This can be a parallel flat or round piece or a single large round rod or tube. The bed should be straight and stiff. Also on it is the tailstock (Fig. 12-1C). It has a center at the same height as the headstock spindle. It can slide and be locked at any position on the bed. A bed long enough to give a capacity of over 30 inches allows table legs to be turned.

Drive at the headstock is made with some form of spur center. It locates the wood and has teeth to dig in (Fig. 12-1D). At the tailstock, there is a plain center (Fig. 12-1E) or a live center that revolves with the wood. Tools are used on a T-rest (Fig. 12-1F). It can be moved about the bed and locked in place with the actual rest adjustable in height and angle.

For bowls and similar large diameter things, the limit of size is determined by the height of the centers above the bed. This can be described by the largest diameter or radius that can be cleared.

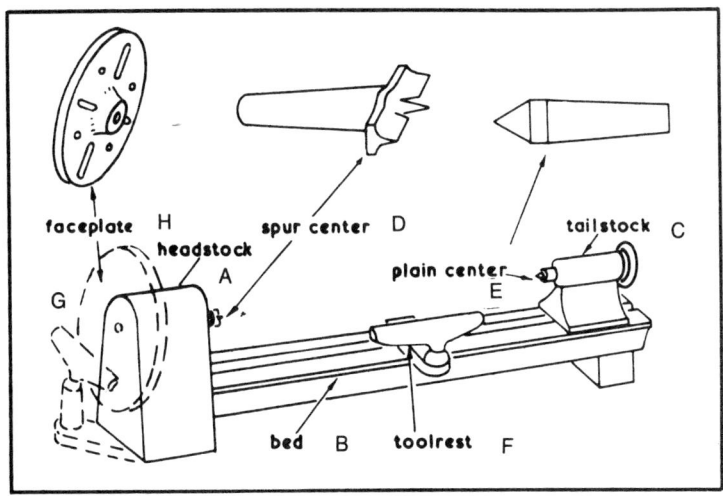

Fig. 12-1. Wood turning lathe is of simple, rigid construction.

Some beds have a gap near the headstock to give a greater clearance, but a better arrangement is to allow for bowls to be turned at the outboard end of the headstock (Fig. 12-1G), with another mounting for the tool rest there. There are several devices for holding shallow large diameter work, but the standard one is a faceplate with many holes for screws (Fig. 12-1H).

Wood turning tools are gouges and chisels. They are longer in both blades and handles than ordinary bench tools. Gouges are the roughing tools. They are also needed for some finishing processes. Chisels are mostly used for smoothing after working to shape with gouges.

Wood turning gouges come in many widths. A ½-inch one will do most general turning, but a ¼-inch one will be needed for small hollows. The end of the tool is ground outside and given a rounded end. Chisels are also made in many widths, but a ½-inch one will suit most purposes. The end is skew and bevelled both sides. Sharpening on the oilstone should be at the ground angle so that there are no second bevels. A parting tool cuts directly into the revolving wood for deep grooves as well as for cutting off.

Calipers (Fig. 12-2A) are needed for checking diameters. A drill chuck to mount in the tailstock (Fig. 12-2B) allows holes to be drilled centrally in turned work. It is possible to use the lathe as a drilling machine for other work as well. This is particularly true if the drill chuck can be mounted on the headstock spindle.

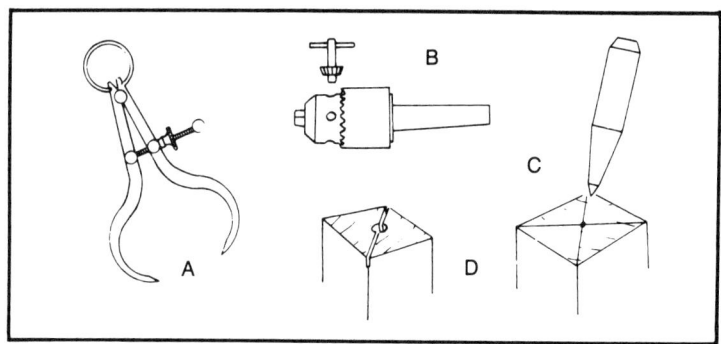

Fig. 12-2. Round work is checked with calipers (A). A tailstock drill chuck (B) makes central holes. Square stock is carefully centered (C) and prepared for the lathe centers (D).

Most of the woods used for cabinetmaking can be turned. The close-grained ones are better than the open-grained ones, and beech turns more easily than oak. Harder woods are better for fine detail. Some softwoods need care, or they will break out.

Wood for turning between centers should be square. Most woods can be turned from square. If there seems much risk of splintering, the corners can be planed off to make it roughly octagonal. Mark the center at each end and make a dot with a center punch (Fig. 12-2C). For a two-prong driving center, there could be a shallow saw cut across the center (Fig. 12-2D). Put the wood in the lathe with the tailstock adjusted to bring its center tightly into the wood. If it is a plain center, put a spot of grease on it. There might be wear at the center during turning, so tighten it occasionally.

Set the tool rest to clear the wood and just below center height. Hold the gouge with one hand on it at the tool rest and the other on the handle. It might be sufficient to have your thumb over the tool rest or you might have to put your hand on top for a heavy cut. Start the lathe and advance the tool to take off the high spots of the wood. Move it along as well as in and aim to reduce the wood to a cylinder. At first you could scrape by pointing the tool towards the center (Fig. 12-3A), but you get a better cut if the tool points more around the curve (Fig. 12-3B). You will also get a better surface if the gouge is tilted towards the direction of cut along the wood so that its side is working with more of a slicing action (Fig. 12-3C).

On the practice piece, the chisel action can be learned on the cylinder. For shaped work, the chisel is not needed until after shaping with gouges. More care is needed in handling a chisel to avoid digging

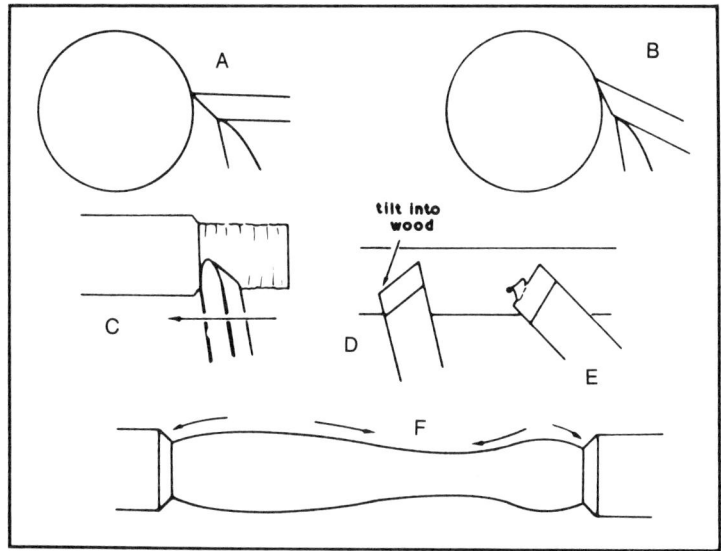

Fig. 12-3. Using a tool near horizontal scrapes (A, B), sloping it up pares, while a sideways movement slices as well. In shaped work, cut toward the thinner parts (C, D, E, F).

in and to keep the cut smooth. Slope the chisel in the direction you want to cut and keep the shorter edge toward you (Fig. 12-3D). It can be turned over and used either way along the wood.

Approach the wood with the bevel of the chisel rubbing on the surface and the center of the cutting edge over the highest part of the circumference. Rock the chisel on the rest so that the cutting edge enters the wood and then begin to slice along (Fig. 12-3E). Use both hands to control the movement and the angle of the tool. It might not matter if the lower corner of the edge enters the wood, but if the top corner does it will dig in and spoil the surface. Aim to always keep the long corner out of the wood. Practice slicing in this way in both directions. Change hands the other way.

There are many decorative spindles with hollows in the length. Get the shape almost to size with a gouge. It is best to use a slicing action toward the thinnest part (Fig. 12-3F). Change to a chisel and slice toward the thinnest part from both directions. If you cut uphill, then stop the lathe and examine the surface. You will see that the fibers tear out and the general finish is rough.

Steps in using the tools to turn a shape are best seen with an example such as a spindle that might make a leg or be one of many in a frame (Fig. 12-4A). Start with a piece of wood an inch or so

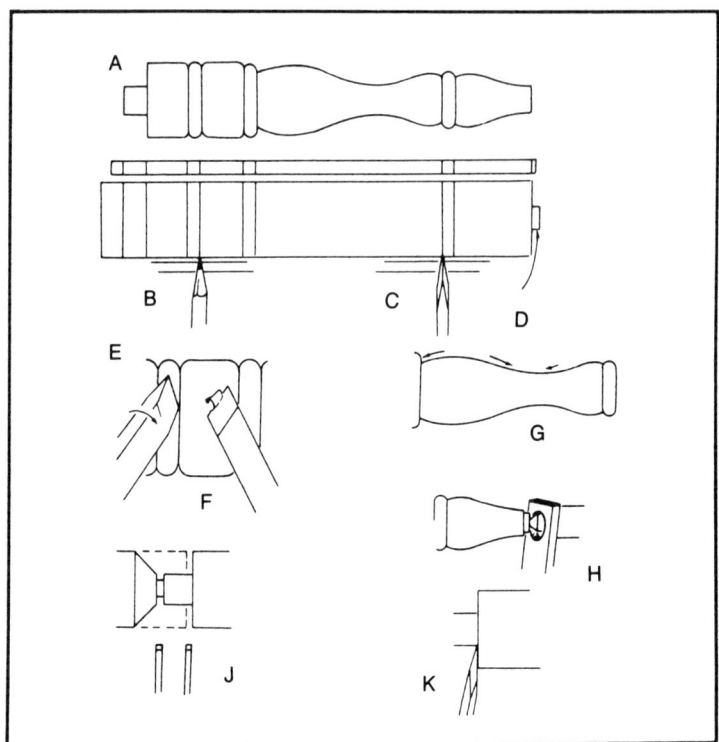

Fig. 12-4. Use a rod to mark matching parts (A, B, C, D). Cut in beads with the edge of a chisel and use it to pare surface smooth (E, F). A parting tool cuts straight in, but edges should be trued with a chisel (G, H, J, K). If a part has to fit a hole, drill a scrap piece of wood for testing.

too long. It helps to have some waste wood at the headstock end. Turn the wood to a parallel cylindrical shape with a gouge. Finish almost to the intended maximum size. Use a rule or a strip of wood with the main measurements on it and a pencil to mark on the rotating wood where the key points are (Fig. 12-4B).

Have the tool rest fairly close to the wood. Use the chisel with the long point downward to cut straight in where there are divisions (Fig. 12-4C). The tailstock end can be trued by cutting straight in with the parting tool (Fig. 12-4D). This can also be used at the other end, but do not go too far or the wood will be weakened and might bend or break during other tool work. It is always best to deal with parts away from the ends first while the ends are large and able to resist strain.

Beads are made by using the short side of the chisel and paring with a curving motion from the center of a bead into the cut (Fig. 12-4E). Do this both ways until you have satisfactory curves. Take off enough with the chisel to remove any of the rough gouge marks. Use the chisel on the parallel parts to smooth them (Fig. 12-4F).

Rough the tapered center part to shape with a gouge. Follow with a chisel and go from high to low (Fig. 12-4G). If the tailstock end is to fit into a hole, drill a test hole (with the bit to be used) in a thin piece of scrap wood and use this to try as you turn to size. If it is large enough, it can hang on the tailstock center (Fig. 12-4H). Otherwise, the tailstock must be withdrawn at intervals so that you can test with it. The dowel at the other end cannot be tested in this way. Instead, take the parting tool in some way at the shoulder and at its end. Then remove some waste with a gouge. Follow by paring with a chisel (Fig. 12-4J). Some of the excess at the end might have to be cut away to allow the chisel to be taken in at the correct angle.

A parting tool leaves a rough surface across the end grain. If it is important that a shoulder be smooth, cut on the waste side of the line with the parting tool. Then use a chisel with its long point downward and one bevel in line with the shoulder (Fig. 12-4K) to cut the end smooth.

Careful work with tools, particularly paring with a chisel that is really sharp, should result in a good surface that only needs a minimum of sanding with a fine grit paper. Much can be done to improve poor work by sanding with coarser grit, but a good turner gets results with his tools and only has a little use for abrasives.

When you are satisfied with the spindle, turn down the bottom to the center, or close to it, and take the parting tool in at the headstock end to cut off the surplus there. For the best end on something where it will show, use the long point of the chisel and reduce the wood progressively until it is quite small. Then remove the wood from the lathe and saw it off so that there is enough left to trim with a chisel and by sanding. For something of a large diameter, such as a bowl or base for a lamp standard, the wood has to be cut circular and mounted on a faceplate. A piece of scrap wood can be mounted with screws on the faceplate. Then the piece to be turned can be glued on with paper in the joint (Fig. 12-5A). After turning, a knife or chisel will prise away the work, then surplus paper can be sanded off. If screw holes in the base will not matter, the screws can go through a piece of plywood into the work (Fig. 12-5B).

Turn the outside of a true circle by scraping with a gouge (Fig. 12-5C). Because the grain will usually be across the disk, trying to cut by sloping the gouge up will cause it to dig in where the grain opposes it. On the face, use the gouge to rough the surface to the shape you want (Fig. 12-5D).

Ordinary turning chisels cannot be used on faceplate work. Instead, use scrapers that are sharpened to an obtuse angle (Fig. 12-5E). The edge should be keen and frequently touched up. Have the tool rest slightly above center and slope the tool downward (Fig. 12-5F), experiment with the angle until the tool takes off fine shavings (not just dust). For heavy work, there are very stout scrapers. For much turning, the ends of ordinary chisel section steel can be ground to shape. Much can be done with a moderately curved end (Fig. 12-5G) and one with a straight end having its corners taken off (Fig. 12-5H).

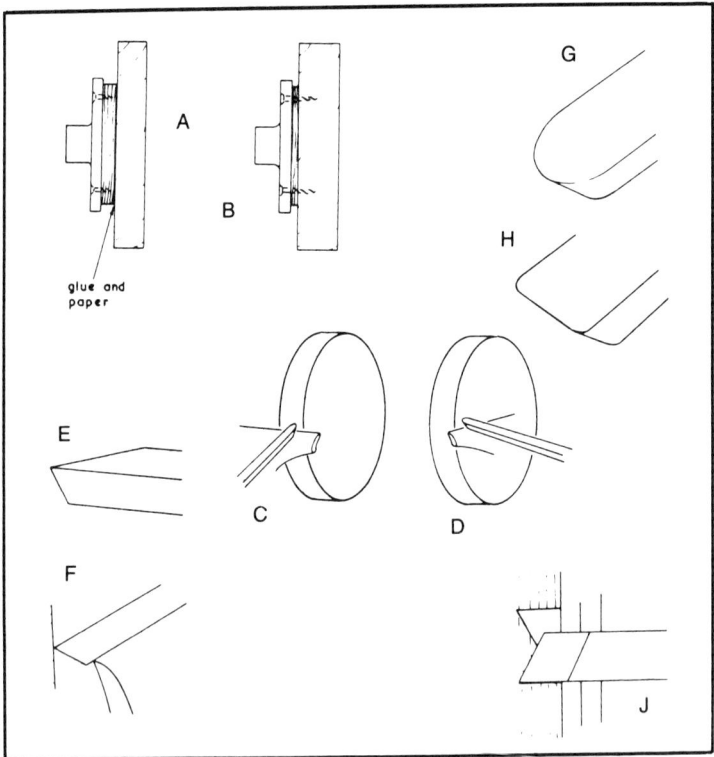

Fig. 12-5. Large discs are turned on a faceplate (A, B, C, D) and surface work is done with scrapers (E, F, G, H, J).

If a hole is needed at the center of a disk, it can be turned with a pointed chisel (Fig. 12-5J). There might have to be more sanding of a base or bowl because of the grain running across causing tearing up at two parts of a circle. If the lathe can be reversed, some of this roughness can be removed with a tool. Otherwise, sanding with progressively finer grits will be required.

Project 13

Firehouse Armchair

Armchairs shaped to fit around the body are sometimes loosely referred to as "Windsor chairs," but the true Windsor chair has an arched back. The firehouse armchair gets its name from its common use in early days in the quarters of volunteer fire departments. There are a great variety, but the specimen shown (Fig. 13-1A) is chosen because it can be made without steaming wood, and because it utilizes some of the lathe turning techniques given in project 12.

Some chairs had flat seats, others were shaped, while others were shaped from back to front, while remaining straight across (Fig. 13-1B). The front edge is straight, the grain is across the seat and the back is a part of a circle (Fig. 13-1C). The seat is the key member of the assembly. Make this first. Locate the leg positions on the underside. On the top, pencil a line around parallel with the edge and position the spindle locations on this. Note there is an even number and spacing is uniform (Fig. 13-1D).

The front legs are upright when viewed from the side, but are splayed when viewed from the front. The rear legs have the same splay as the front legs when viewed from the front, but from the side they are seen to have considerable splay towards the rear (Fig. 13-1E). It is difficult to arrive at the exact sizes of the legs, so the tops are turned with parallel parts to adjust in the seat holes, while the bottoms are arranged so that final trimming to length will not affect their appearance (Fig. 13-1F). In this case, the front legs are decorated with beads, but the rear legs are plainer.

The spindles are turned with thicker centers and there may be beads to match the front legs (Fig. 13-1G). In effect, the under assembly and seat may be regarded as a stool and can be put together without reference to the parts above the seat. This can be done before proceeding with the arms and spindles, if you wish.

The combined arms and back is laminated with two or three thicknesses. The shape must match the seat, and the inner edge should be just within the outline of the seat (Fig. 13-2A). Use any convenient lengths of wood. Let them butt together and arrange joints to come at different places in each layer (Fig. 13-2B). Cut each piece to shape with a little to spare. Glue the part together and put them under pressure until set. After that you can treat the laminated part as a single piece of wood. Trim its profile, but do not do any cross-sectional shaping at this stage.

Transfer the spindle locations from the seat to the arm. The spindles will flare out slightly. Let the front pair flare in the width, but be upright when viewed from the side, then space the hole positions for the others around the centerline of the arm piece (Fig. 13-2C).

The eight spindles are all the same. Allow a little excess length and keep the ends parallel and to the hole size, so they will still fit if trimmed to length.

The armchair can be completed at this stage, but many chairs were given an extension backrest. A modern method of making would be to laminate many thin pieces of wood around a mold, but the older glues were not suitable for this method, so the backrests were built up by laminating more flat pieces in a similar way to the making of the arm piece (Fig. 13-2D). This can be worked with spokeshave and plane to a comfortable section to mount on top of the arm piece (Fig. 13-2E), with dowels or screws from below.

This method of mounting does not give high support to the back and another method of mounting the backrest is to use short spindles located above and between the main spindles (Fig. 13-2F). These are turned with dowel ends (Fig. 13-2G) and stand upright between the two parts.

The front ends of the arms should be well rounded. Most of the rest of the shape should also have a rounded section. The holes for the spindles connecting to the seat will have to be drilled at angles judged by eye, with appropriate adjustment later with gouge and chisel if necessary.

When the arm is to be attached to the seat, have all the spindle ends glued and lightly inserted in place in the seat. Bring the arm

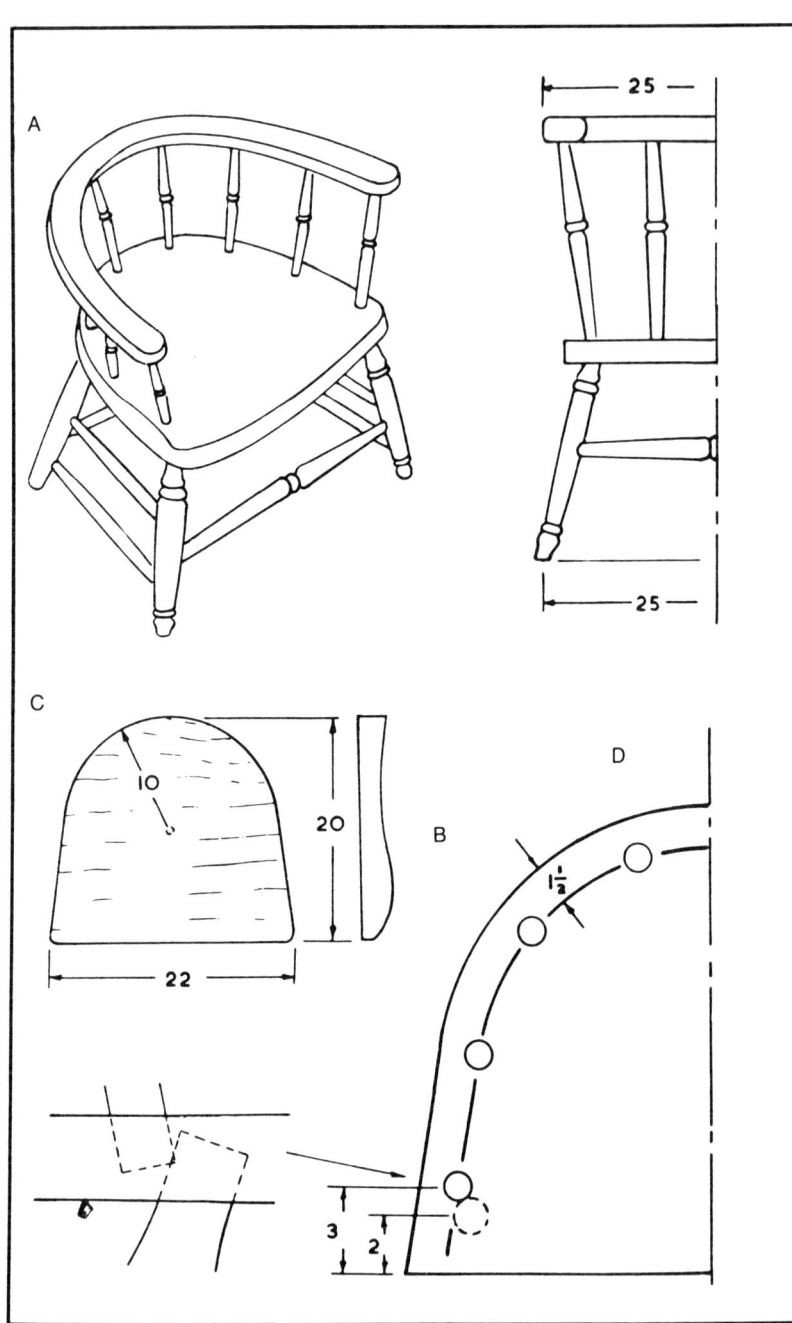

Fig. 13-1. Firehouse armchair dimensions.

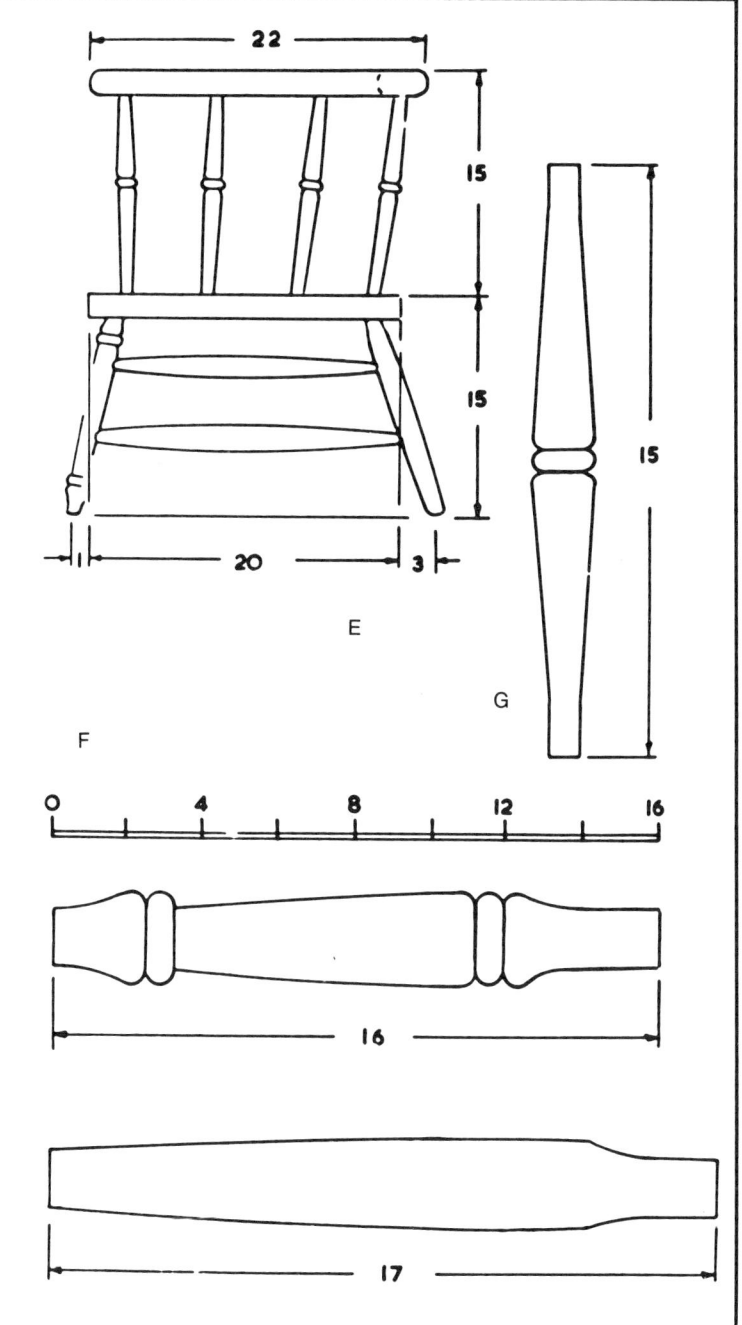

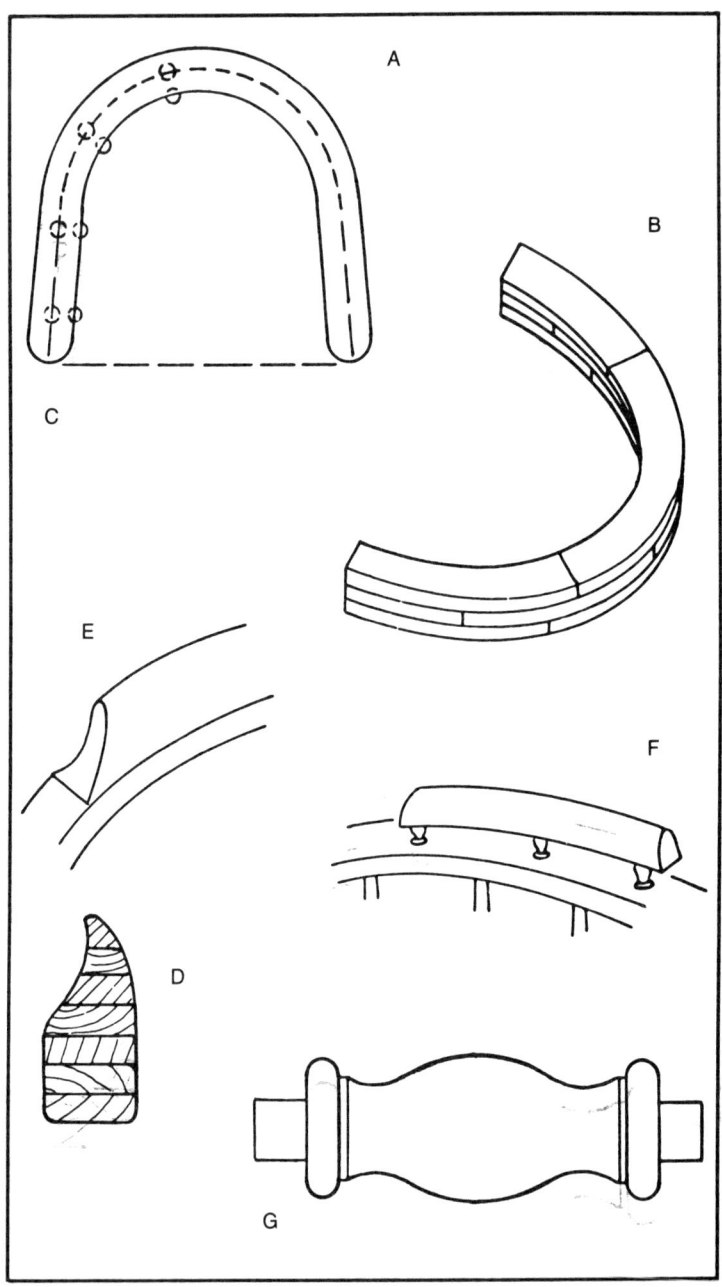

Fig. 13-2. Back and arms of firehouse armchair.

into place and get the spindle ends located in their holes. Use a piece of scrap wood under a hammer or mallet to work around the arm a little at a time driving the parts together. When all of the spindles have entered a short distance, check that the arm is parallel with the seat and the assembly when viewed from the front is not flaring more one way than the other. Continue driving progressively around the arm until all the joints are fully closed and the chair is seen to be symmetrical.

Materials List for Firehouse Armchair

1 Arm from	$5 \times 180 \times 5/8$
4 Legs	$2 \times 17 \times 2$
8 Spindles	$1 1/4 \times 15 \times 1 1/4$
7 Rails	$1 1/2 \times 22 \times 1 1/2$
1 Back from	$5 \times 100 \times 5/8$
1 Seat	$20 \times 22 \times 1 1/2$
3 Back spindles	$1 1/2 \times 5 \times 1 1/2$

Project 14

Cheval Mirror

A mirror that shows the full length of the viewer does not have to be very big, providing it can be tilted, but it has to be a reasonable size and mirror glass can be quite heavy. The mirror supports have to be stout enough to remain rigid. Better mirrors, particularly if one is obtained from an old piece of furniture, will be found to be thick glass. Obviously, it is the condition of the "silvering" on the back which is important. Handle a mirror carefully and avoid putting it down where there could be a risk of damaging the back.

Because the size of the stand depends on the mirror size, get that first and plan the other sizes to suit it. The frame has to be supported between the posts with fittings that allow the mirror to tilt while providing enough friction to keep it at any angle. There are several types., A simple one has a deep V-shaped socket to fit to the post and a part with a domed extension to drop into the socket. That way it is possible to lift the mirror frame off. Because the clearance for a fitting at each side governs the spacing of the posts, these fittings should also be obtained before starting on the woodwork. The design shown in Fig. 14-1 suits a mirror about 18 inches by 42 inches and the sections of wood specified will serve as a guide if dimensions have to be modified.

The parts can be made with straight lines and square edges, but the necessarily fairly stout sections can be lightened in appearance by using curves and rounding the corners of sections.

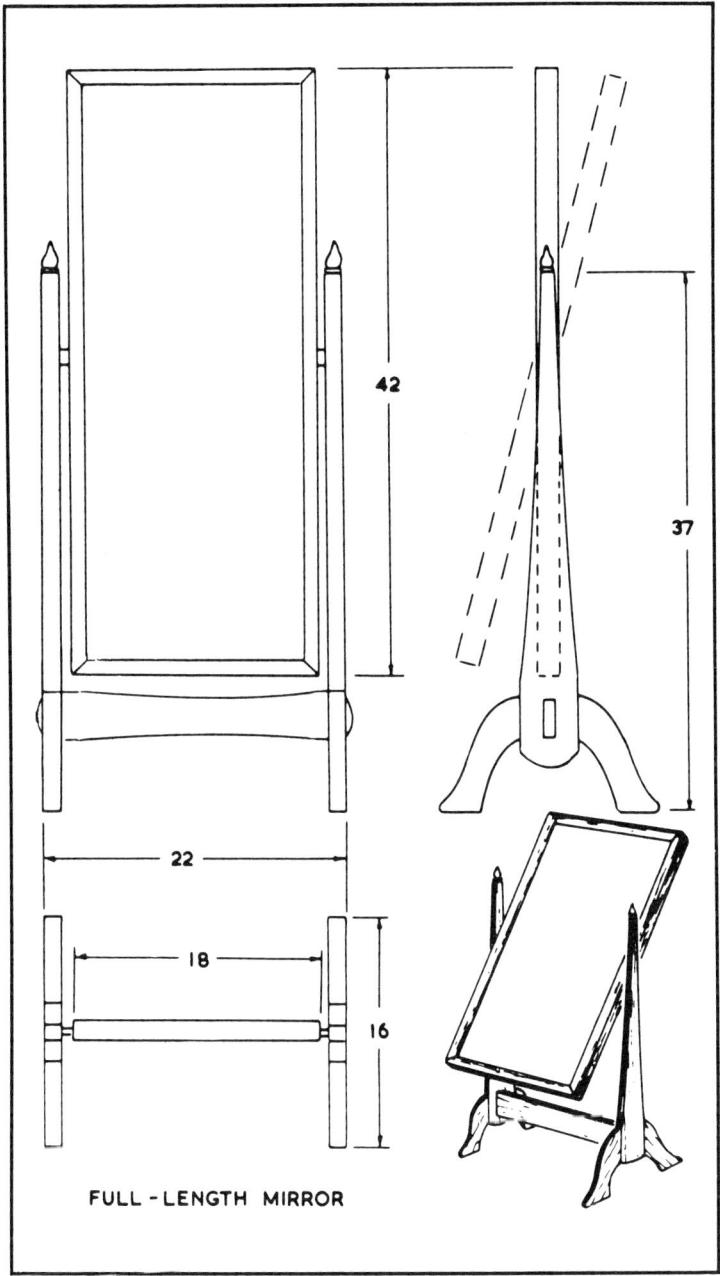

Fig. 14-1. Large tilting mirror shows a person full-length.

The frame around the glass has a deep section for stiffness and the back is stiff enough to relieve the glass of strain (Fig. 14-2A). The sections of the rabbets should suit the glass and plywood, but allow for a piece of cloth, thin plastic foam or even paper, between the plywood and the back of the mirror.

The visible part of the frame can be molded in several ways, depending on the equipment available, but the curved section shown here can be worked with ordinary planes followed by sanding. The plywood back should be made a good fit in the frame, but there can be a little clearance around the glass so that it is the plywood and not the glass that keeps the frame in shape. Whatever finish is used for the rest of the woodwork, paint the inside of the glass rabbet black to avoid an unattractive reflection around the edges.

The plywood back screwed in place provides stiffness and strength, but the corners of the frame should have joints stronger than would be acceptable for a picture frame. A mitered bridle joint is suitable (Fig. 14-2B). For clarity, this is shown on wood of square section, but it can be used with the rounded section and any other except a deep molding. Alternatively, cut simple miters. Then drill across them at different levels for thin dowels, glued in and planed level (Fig. 14-2C).

Arrange the pivot point slightly above halfway up each side. About 1 inch above the middle should suit a 42-inch depth. If the pivot is exactly on the point of balance, the mirror will swing too easily.

Each post has a parallel lower part (Fig. 14-2D). Then it tapers to a square end above the pivot. Instead of a straight taper, appearance is improved if each is slightly hollow. a ¼-inch greatest depth in the length is enough. The top can be rounded or a turned finial can be added. These can be bought, but a suitable design to turn is shown in (Fig. 14-2E).

The rail provides stiffness in a crosswise direction and should be securely joined to the posts. Dowel joints might not be strong enough. It would be better to shoulder the rail ends and have a tenon through each post and then round its exposed end (Fig. 14-2F). If the posts are hollowed along their tapers, give the edges of the rail matching hollowing.

Draw a leg full size (Fig. 14-2G). Make a template or use one leg as a pattern for the others. Arrange the grain the long way. The joints to the posts can be mortise and tenon (Fig. 14-2H) or dowels (Fig. 14-2J). In both cases, there will be difficulty in pulling the joints tight if the legs are fully finished before assembly. It is better to

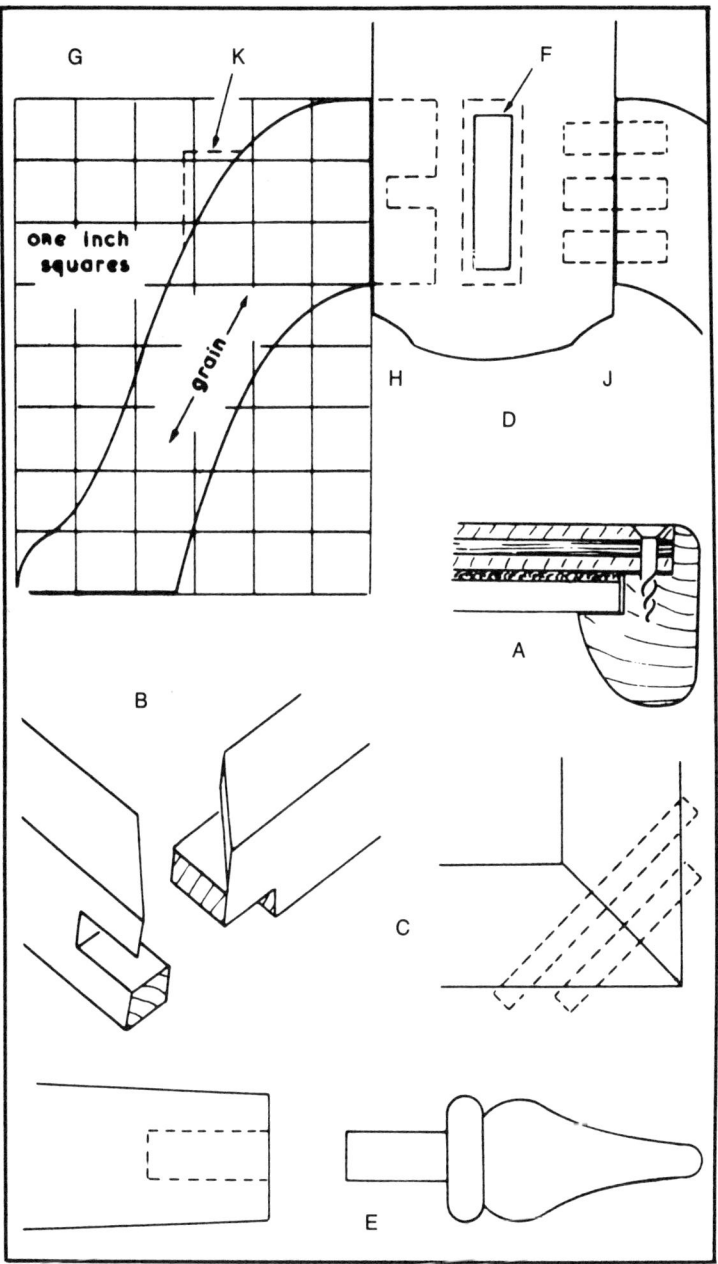

Fig. 14-2. Details of full-length mirror: (A) frame; (B) mitered bridle joint; (C) planed level; (D, E, F) parallel post; (G) leg; (H) mortise and tenon; (J) dowel; (K) projection.

leave on a small projection for clamping (Fig. 14-2K) while the rest of the outline is finished to size and rounded. Leave just the small area to deal with after the projections have been cut off.

Assemble the pair of posts with their feet and see that they match and will stand level. Then join them with the rail. Check squareness carefully and leave the assembly for glue to set while it is standing on a level surface.

Finishing is most easily done before the mirror goes into the frame, but a trial assembly with a few screws in the back is advisable.

Materials List for Full-Length Mirror.

2	frame sides	$1\frac{1}{2} \times 45 \times 1$
2	frame ends	$1\frac{1}{2} \times 20 \times 1$
1	frame back	$20 \times 45 \times \frac{3}{8}$ plywood
2	posts	$4 \times 36 \times 1\frac{1}{4}$
4	legs	$3\frac{1}{2} \times 11 \times 1\frac{1}{4}$
1	rail	$3 \times 24 \times 1\frac{1}{4}$
2	finials	$1\frac{1}{4} \times 4 \times \frac{1}{4}$

Project 15

Tallboy

This tallboy is the last and most ambitious project in our book, utilizing many of the special woodworking techniques presented in earlier projects.

A truly elegant piece of furniture, this traditional design is made in two sections, allowing easy dismantling and moving. Several variations are shown (Fig. 15-1), both with and without a crown molding. The crown molding goes with a fairly ornate treatment and patterned brass drawer pulls. With a more severe modern theme, a much simpler top would be appropriate.

The example described here is reminiscent of the 18th century (Fig. 15-1D). It can easily be adapted to a reduced form or simplified in many details.

The pedestal could be on cabriole legs (Fig. 15-2A) as already described, but shorter legs give greater storage space (Fig. 15-2B). Leave enough clearance for cleaning the floor. The legs are like dumpy cabriole legs with square sections cut from solid blocks and with ears attached (Fig. 15-2C). The frame is made up like that of a table and preferably with a bead along the lower edge and with a rabbet at the top to locate the main chest (Fig. 15-2D). The assembly will probably be strong enough as it is, but if necessary glue blocks in the corners.

The main chest is flat-fronted. Some chests have the drawer fronts curved, but that means cutting thicker wood to waste. If there is much bowing, the surfaces should be veneered. There are two

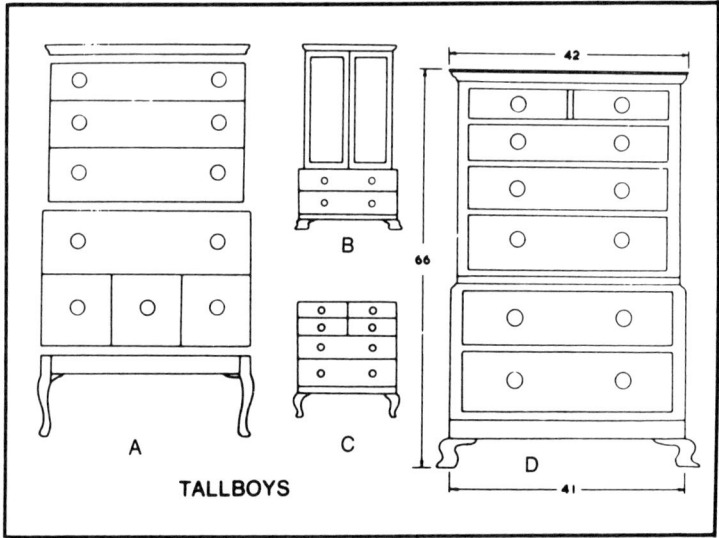

Fig. 15-1. Tallboys may take several forms and are usually sectional.

deep drawers. Decoration is provided by having the drawer fronts overlapping and molded and there are molded pillar effects at the side (Fig. 15-3A). Hidden parts need not be of such good quality wood as the face wood.

The ends of the chest can be made by gluing boards to make up a sufficient width or plywood faced with matching veneer could be framed (Fig. 15-3B). Rabbet the rear edges for the plywood back. At the front, the two pillar pieces (Fig. 15-3C) could be plain, but they look better if worked to a bead similar to that on the plinth, but carried around and the ends bevelled.

Glue the pillars to the ends. A good glued joint should be satisfactory, but extra strength can be provided by secret-slot screwing the joints as well.

The strips that go across the chest are notched around the pillars at the front and come level with the bottoms of the rabbets at the back. Shorter pieces fit between them and act as drawer runners (Fig. 15-3D). Join these parts with short tenons. Put drawer guides level with the edges of the pillars (Fig. 15-3E). They also provide strength in the joints. Top and bottom assemblies are the same as those between the drawers.

Underneath the bottom, arrange locating strips so that the chest fits into the pedestal (Fig. 15-3F). But do not make it so tight that it cannot be lifted out.

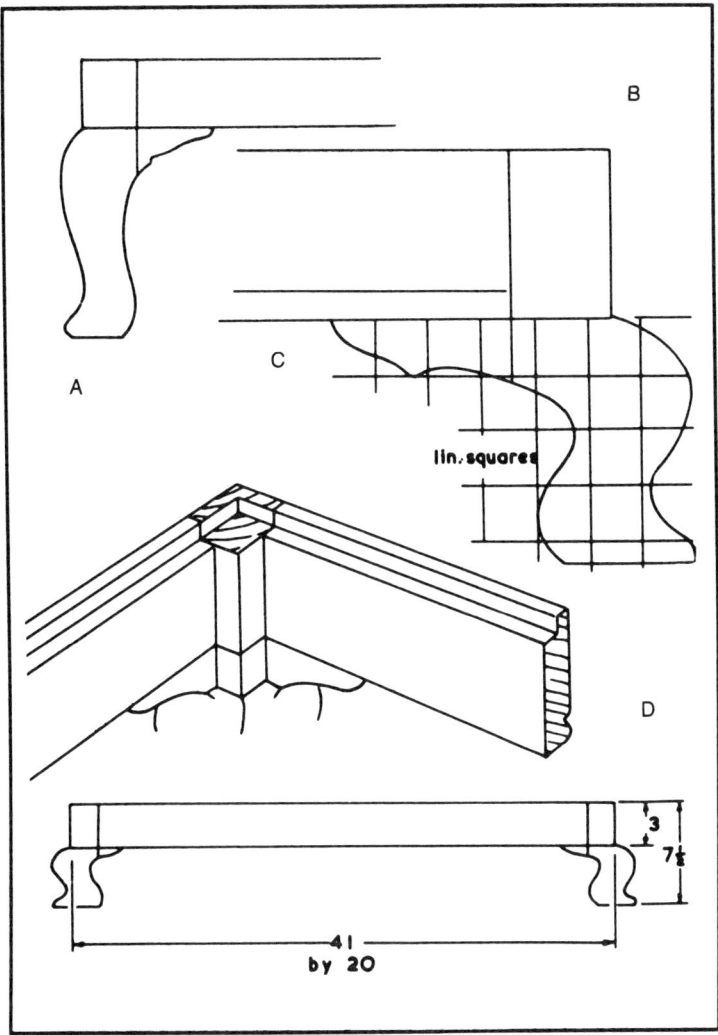

Fig. 15-2. Bottom of tallboy (A, B, C) is built up like a table frame (D).

If the chest is to be finished without the upper part and its top will be exposed, the top can be made from solid wood like a table top, or it can be of framed plywood with a veneered surface forming a central panel. If there is to be a top chest or a glass-fronted cupboard, the top of the lower chest need only be framed around. To seal it, there could be a plywood panel set in a plowed groove. Miter the corners. Mold the front and end edges. A simple pattern is shown in Fig. 15-3G, but other sections are possible. Screw these

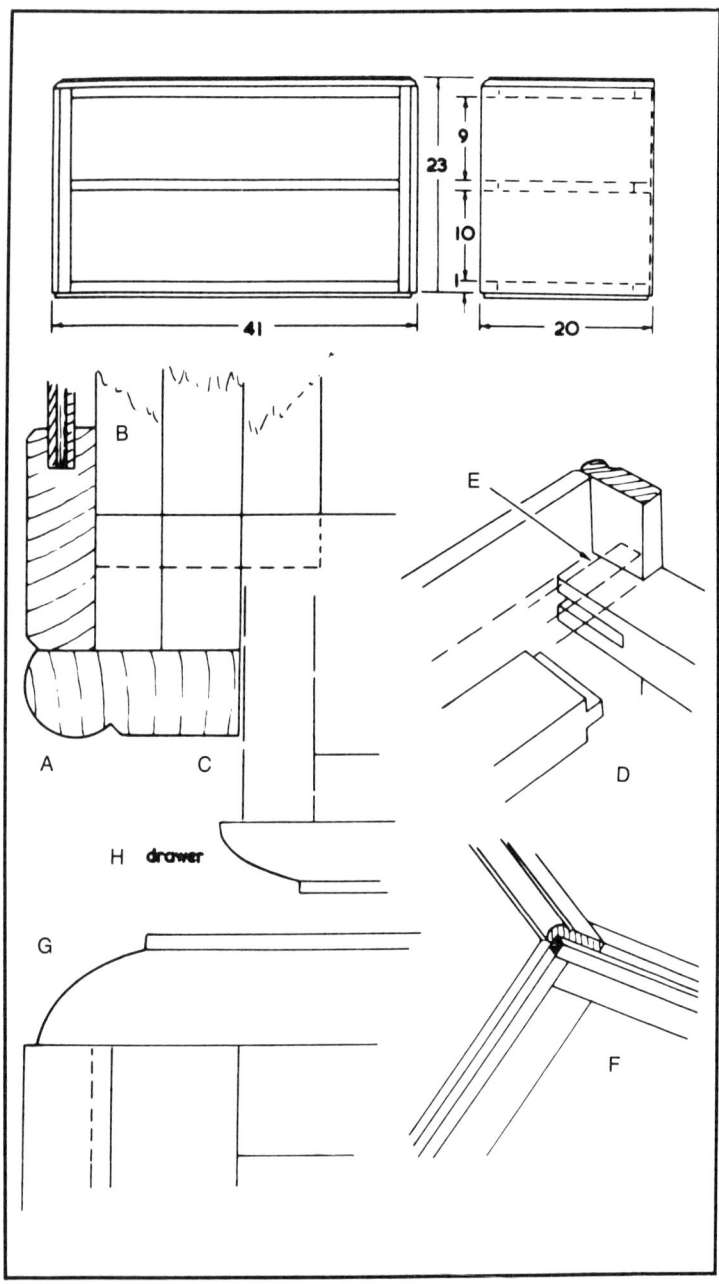

Fig. 15-3. Main part of tallboy has pillars at sides (A, B, C) and the drawer fronts overlap (D, E, F, G).

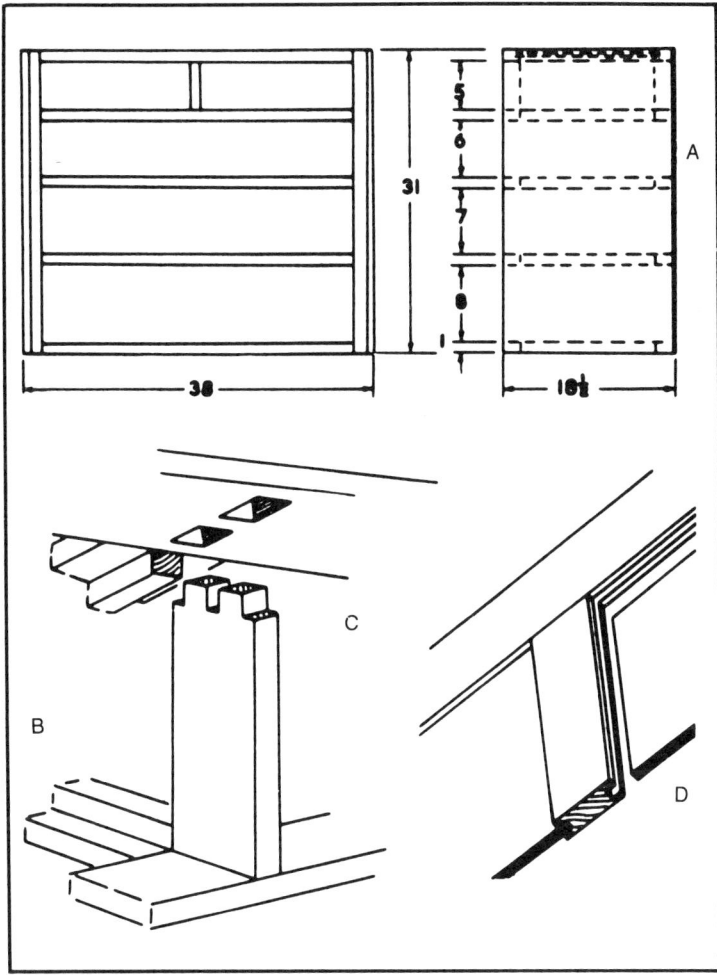

Fig. 15-4. Upper part has tapered drawer widths (A, B, C) and a division between top drawers (D).

parts to the framing on the top of the chest. If it is set back, see that the margin is parallel and the same all round.

The upper chest (Fig. 15-4A) is made in the same way as the main chest, but its sizes allow for it being set in an equal amount from the sides and front of the main chest.

For the division between the top drawers, tenon in a wide runner in the frame below and another in the frame above to act as a kicker (Fig. 15-4B). At the front and back, put uprights between the frames and tenoned into them (Fig. 15-4C). Then put guides between them.

It would be sufficient to put thin plywood on top of this part of the chest to keep out dust, but nailing it on might not be considered good cabinetmaking and it would be better to let it into grooves when the top frame parts are assembled (Fig. 15-4D).

The type of crown molding depends on what molding can be cut with available equipment or bought already shaped. To give the tallboy a balanced appearance, it should broaden at the top. Make a frame of the same size as the top of the chest (Fig. 15-5A). Around this, form a shallow box on to which can go a top frame (Fig. 15-5B). Arrange the lower edge of the box to overlap the chest slightly to locate the parts. Both of these pieces can be shaped on their edges to form part of the molding so that they blend in with the molding proper which fits between them (Fig. 15-5C). There is no need to carry the molding around the back, but miter the front corners neatly.

To prevent movement, the upper chest can be joined to the lower part with four screws and the crown molding can be held in the same way. Do not use glue. The parts can be disassembled whenever necessary.

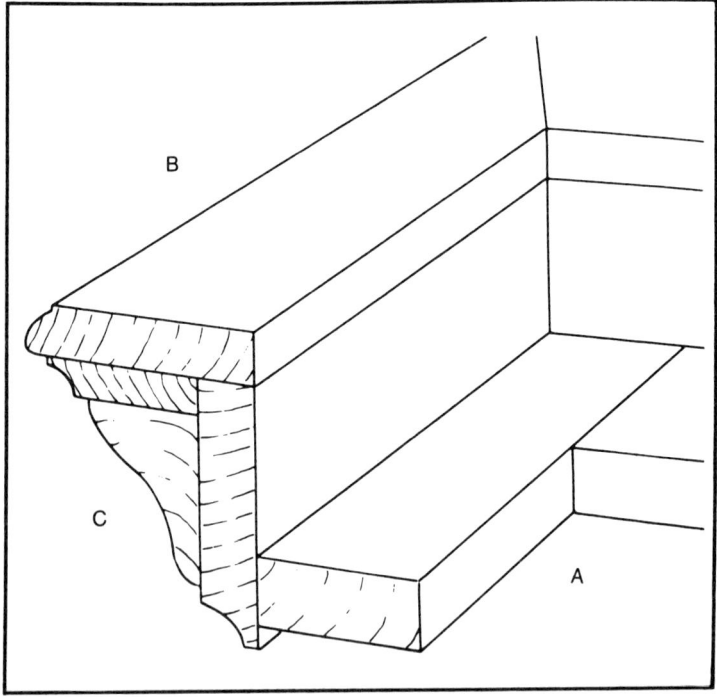

Fig. 15-5. Molded top (A) is built up to rest on the top section (B) of drawers (C).

The drawers are made in the usual way, with dovetails and plywood bottoms, but there are overlapping fronts. Make the drawers with the main fronts level with the fronts of the chest parts, but make false fronts to overlap at sides and tops by ¼ inch (Fig. 15-3H). Mold the false fronts to match the molding used on the top of the main chest or that of the crown. Attach the false fronts with screws from inside. See that the edges of the drawers finish level with each other when all drawers are pushed home and there are no parts out of parallel. It is advisable to fit the false fronts and do whatever trimming is necessary before molding their edges.

This type of furniture looks best with decorative brass drawer pulls rather than wooden ones. It is the pair of top drawers which govern the handle spacing. The handles must be central across each drawer, and the other drawer pulls should be vertically below them. On each drawer, locate the handles slightly above center.

The plywood backs are glued and screwed or nailed in. The drawers should not quite reach them, but overlapping drawer fronts will act as stops and prevent the drawers going too far.

Separate the parts for finishing. Parts that are normally hidden can be given a single coat of varnish to reduce water absorption. When staining and polishing the exterior, be careful to treat each part similarly so that there is a uniform appearance when the tallboy is assembled.

Materials List for Tallboy

Pedestal

2 frames	$3 \times 42 \times 1$
2 frames	$3 \times 20 \times 1$
4 legs	$3½ \times 8 \times 3½$
8 leg ears	$1 \times 3½ \times 1$

Main chest

2 ends or	$20 \times 23 \times ⅝$
¼-inch plywood framed with	$2 \times ⅝$
6 strips	$2 \times 41 \times 1$
6 strips	$2¼ \times 18 \times 1$
4 drawer guides	$¾ \times 20 \times ¾$
2 locating strips	$½ \times 41 \times ½$
2 locating strips	$½ \times 20 \times ½$
1 back	$20 \times 41 \times ¼$ plywood

1 top	20 × 41 × 1
or	
¼ plywood framed with	2 × 1
2 pillar pieces	2 × 23 × 1

Upper chest

2 ends	18½ × 32 × ⅝
or	
¼ plywood framed with	2 × ⅝
10 strips	2 × 38 × 1
10 strips	2¼ × 18 × 1
12 drawer guides	¾ × 19 × ¾
1 back	31 × 38 × ¼ plywood
1 top	18 × 30 × ½ plywood
2 pillar pieces	2 × 31 × 1
2 drawer dividers	2 × 8 × 1

Crown molding

2 frame pieces	2 × 38 × 1
2 frame pieces	2 × 19 × 1
1 top frame	3 × 43 × ⅝
2 top frames	3 × 22 × ⅝
molding from	2½ × 80 × 1½

Drawers

2 first fronts	5 × 19 × ⅝
2 first fronts	5½ × 19 × ⅝
2 backs	4½ × 19 × ⅝
4 sides	5 × 19 × ⅝
2 bottoms	19 × 19 × ¼ plywood
1 second front	6 × 36 × ⅝
1 second front	6½ × 36 × ⅝
1 back	6 × 36 × ⅝
2 sides	6 × 19 × ⅝
1 third front	7 × 36 × ⅝
1 third front	7½ × 36 × ⅝
1 back	7 × 36 × ⅝
2 sides	7 × 19 × ⅝
1 fourth front	8 × 36 × ⅝
1 fourth front	8½ × 36 × ⅝
1 back	8 × 36 × ⅝
2 sides	8 × 19 × ⅝

1 fifth front	$9 \times 38 \times 5/8$
1 fifth front	$9 1/2 \times 38 \times 5/8$
1 back	$9 \times 38 \times 5/8$
2 sides	$9 \times 19 \times 5/8$
1 sixth drawer front	$10 \times 38 \times 5/8$
1 sixth drawer front	$10 1/2 \times 38 \times 5/8$
1 back	$10 \times 38 \times 5/8$
2 sides	$10 \times 19 \times 5/8$
5 bottoms	$20 \times 40 \times 1/4$ plywood

Index

B
beads, 67
beveling, 15
blind dovetails, 57
blind lap dovetail, 55
bookcase, 14-17

C
chest, dovetail, 58
cheval mirror, 76-80
chisels, 63
crown molding, 86
cushions, 43

D
dadoes, 4, 14
doll carriage, 8-13
dovetail chest, 58-61
dovetail joints, 48-57, 58
doweled joint, 79
drawers, 55, 84, 85

F
firehouse armchair, 70-75

G
go-kart, 27-33
gouges, 63

H
half blind dovetail, 49
headstock, 62
hidden dovetails, 55
housed and mitered dovetail, 57

L
ladder for swing set, 36
lap dovetail, 49, 53
lathe turning, 62-69

M
mirror, 76-80
mitered bridle joint, 79
mortise and tenon joint, 79

P
parson's bench, 4-7
parting tools, 67
pins, 48
plinth, 16

R
rabbeting, 15, 16
riding crane, 21-26
    moving parts diagram for, 25
rocking chair, 43-47

S
scooter, 18-20
seat joints, 45
secret dovetails, 57
sliding board for swing set, 37-42
spindle, 65, 70
stopped dovetails, 49, 54, 55
swing set, 34-42
    ladder for, 36
    sliding board for, 37-42

T
tails, 48
tailstock, 63
tallboy, 81-89
through dovetails, 51
toys
    doll carriage, 8-13
    go-kart, 27-33
    riding crane, 21-26
    scooter, 18-20
    swing set, 34-42
    twisting acrobat, 1-3
twisting acrobat, 1-3